T0295758

The Innovator's Imperative

The Innovator's Imperative
Rapid Technology Adoption for Digital Transformation

Stephen J. Andriole

Thomas Cox

Kaung M. Khin

CRC Press
Taylor & Francis Group
Boca Raton London New York

CRC Press is an imprint of the
Taylor & Francis Group, an **informa** business
AN AUERBACH BOOK

CRC Press
Taylor & Francis Group
6000 Broken Sound Parkway NW, Suite 300
Boca Raton, FL 33487-2742

© 2018 by Taylor & Francis Group, LLC
CRC Press is an imprint of Taylor & Francis Group, an Informa business

No claim to original U.S. Government works

Printed on acid-free paper

International Standard Book Number-13: 978-1-1387-1355-0 (Hardback)

This book contains information obtained from authentic and highly regarded sources. Reasonable efforts have been made to publish reliable data and information, but the author and publisher cannot assume responsibility for the validity of all materials or the consequences of their use. The authors and publishers have attempted to trace the copyright holders of all material reproduced in this publication and apologize to copyright holders if permission to publish in this form has not been obtained. If any copyright material has not been acknowledged please write and let us know so we may rectify in any future reprint.

Except as permitted under U.S. Copyright Law, no part of this book may be reprinted, reproduced, transmitted, or utilized in any form by any electronic, mechanical, or other means, now known or hereafter invented, including photocopying, microfilming, and recording, or in any information storage or retrieval system, without written permission from the publishers.

For permission to photocopy or use material electronically from this work, please access www.copyright. com (http://www.copyright.com/) or contact the Copyright Clearance Center, Inc. (CCC), 222 Rosewood Drive, Danvers, MA 01923, 978-750-8400. CCC is a not-for-profit organization that provides licenses and registration for a variety of users. For organizations that have been granted a photocopy license by the CCC, a separate system of payment has been arranged.

Trademark Notice: Product or corporate names may be trademarks or registered trademarks, and are used only for identification and explanation without intent to infringe.

**Visit the Taylor & Francis Web site at
http://www.taylorandfrancis.com**

**and the CRC Press Web site at
http://www.crcpress.com**

Contents

Executive Summary

Three names often come to mind when corporate executives and managers think about technology adoption: (1) Clayton Christensen, (2) Geoffrey Moore and (3) Everett Rogers. If they cannot remember the names, they almost always remember *The Innovator's Dilemma*, *Crossing the Chasm* and the technology adoption life cycle described in Rogers' *Diffusion of Innovations*. When these perspectives on technology adoption were presented in the twentieth century, they were insightful and provocative. But today, the insights are not nearly as relevant as they were in the twentieth century.

In the 1990s and even into the twenty-first century, everyone was appropriately intrigued with Clayton Christensen's *The Innovator's Dilemma* and how *good* companies can lose competitive advantage by failing to adopt emerging or disruptive technologies fast enough to maintain or expand their market position (Christensen, 1997).

But even before Christensen's manifesto, Geoffrey Moore argued in *Crossing the Chasm* (Moore, 1991) that technology adoption was often trapped between two phases of the technology adoption life cycle, between *early adopters* and the *early majority*, resulting in a gap (the *chasm*) between how companies see the advantages of technology adoption to fuel their product development, sales and profitability.

Moore's work was anchored in the well-known technology life cycle developed by Everett Rogers in 1962, which recognized five phases of technology adoption: (1) Innovators, (2) early adopters, (3) the early majority, (4) the late majority and (5) the laggards (Rogers, 1962). Moore focused on how high technology marketers could cross the chasm to sell new technology to companies vetting opportunities for digital transformation—though back then no one called technology-driven change *digital transformation*. Other names were used, including *business process reengineering*, *business process management*, *continuous improvement* and even just plain *strategic management*.

All three explanations of technology adoption were *true* at the time, but are much less relevant today—especially for companies committed to digital transformation.

What happened?

The pace of technology change accelerated, hypercompetition grew, opportunities for business model disruption exploded and the arrival of comprehensive cloud delivery all challenged anything traditional or conventional, especially as it impacted the adoption of digital technology—and especially anything with origins in the twentieth century. In fact, the data discussed here challenges every aspect of business technology strategy. Companies have abandoned decades-long approaches to business requirements analysis, technology adoption, corporate governance and entire organizational structures, and replaced it all with technology-driven strategy. The survey and interview data we collected in 2016–2017 indicate that major changes have already begun.

What changed?

Put quite simply, the *innovator's imperative* suggests that to remain competitive all companies should adopt emerging and disruptive technologies as quickly as possible, and in many cases, immediately. The data suggest that companies have all but abandoned the old requirements analysis and modeling *best practices* of the twentieth century. Companies have also ignored the chasm and jumped across adoption phases without regard to any *phasing* whatsoever. Companies have also become immediate and early technology adopters chasing technologies that might impact existing—*and create whole new*—business models and processes. Phased technology adoption is all but gone.

The results reported here are based on 5 years of research conducted at Villanova School of Business, Villanova University, in Villanova,

Pennsylvania. The overarching hypothesis was that companies no longer adopt technology in any sort of phased way and the days when anyone worried about *crossing the chasm* are long gone: the *innovator's dilemma* has become the *innovator's imperative*.

We confirmed the hypothesis.

We learned that companies have abandoned their obsession with requirements and have endorsed a technology-first/requirements-second approach to technology adoption. We learned that companies focused on digital transformation often adopt emerging technologies immediately. We also learned that technology is driving business strategy and that companies are rethinking and reorganizing their technology organizations, especially the governance that determines how and why technology investments are made.

Phase 1 of the research was *conceptual* and described in *Ready Technology: Fast Tracking New Business Technologies* (Andriole, 2014a). The *concept* was simple: companies no longer conduct elaborate requirements analyses as part of the technology adoption process. Instead, companies immediately pilot and deploy emerging technologies without knowing exactly what problems the technologies might solve.

iPads were deployed immediately after they were introduced. Thousands were sold before corporate information technology (IT) groups could declare them *nonstandard* and *unsecure*. The same companies immediately found developers to write *iPad* applications that made their marketing teams more agile. Corporate IT chased them around, but at the end of the day everyone got to keep their *iPads*, and IT declared them *safe—well after deployment*. Fast, creative deployments legitimized *iPads* as solutions to an array of yet-to-be-discovered problems.

Another example: once it was possible to listen to all flavors of social conversations, companies quickly found listening partners (like Radian6 [before and after its acquisition by Salesforce.com] and Crimson Hexagon) and started mining social data about what their customers liked and disliked about their products and services, and the products and services of their competitors. There was no need for corporate IT to get involved. Multiple corporate functions within countless business units—marketing, risk management, brand management and competitor intelligence, among others—all availed themselves of *social business intelligence.* Brand managers did not wait for the listening technology to further mature or the listening process to be perfected. They just signed listening contracts and began to examine the social conversation. Sometimes they told *IT* about these contracts, but sometimes they keep them secret.

The bring-your-own-device (BYOD) to work delivery model also gained momentum *immediately* after it was described by industry gurus, creative companies and even a few academics. Countless companies launched pilots to determine the strengths and weaknesses of the delivery model even before anyone gave the model a name. The idea is simple enough. Since employees have their favorite machines and software applications—and are most productive when they use *personal technology*—and since many companies would love to reduce and eventually eliminate the expensive employee technology benefit—pilots were launched first under the corporate radar and then with great fanfare. BYOD is now a formal movement led by CFOs CIOs and CEOs who like the idea of letting people use whatever technology they want—especially if it reduces technology costs.

Immediately-deployed *iPads*, social media and BYOD. All new technologies and technology delivery models—and all ready for *immediate* deployment.

Twenty-first century technology adoption behavior challenges the twentieth-century phased adoption models that were so popular among technology buyers, especially traditional technology buyers in large organizations. The technology adoption curve originally developed by Everett Rogers (1962) describes a process by which companies vet technology investment decisions. *Innovators* are the earliest adopters; *laggards* are the slowest.

As Figure ES.1 suggests, the percentages are interesting, especially because only 16% are ready technology adopters (the innovators and early adopters), 68% are part of the early/late majority adopters and 16% are laggards. If we look at the adoption of *iPads*, social media and BYOD alone, we see immediate technology adoption rates: *Venture-Beat* (2012) reported that 93% of Fortune 100 companies adopted *iPads* immediately after they were introduced.

The *iPad* adoption rate is unprecedented—or is it? If more and more technologies immediately find their way into more and more companies, what *is* the trajectory of *new* technology adoption?

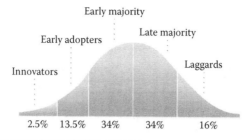

Figure ES.1 The technology adoption curve. (From Rogers, E.M., *Diffusion of Innovations*, Free Press, New York, 1962.)

The new emerging/disruptive technology adoption curve is predicated on technology capability. The conventional assumption is that technology evolves at a pace that justifies phased adoption. Early deployments are assumed to be risky—but potentially high payoff—because the technology is likely not fully baked. Later adoption is safer, especially if a company is part of the *early* or *late* majority (the 68%), and has experience that justifies their approach to technology adoption, that is, they haven't *suffered* because they were *late* or *punished* because they were *early*.

The adoption curve also assumes up-front requirements due diligence where business requirements are well understood and well defined before candidate technologies are vetted. *This is the essence of the old technology adoption curve: requirements-first/technology-second.* Many of us tried to perfect the *requirements-first/technology-second* adoption model (Andriole, 1987, 1992, 1996). The business technology field itself devoted countless articles, books and conferences on the *requirements problem*, *business technology alignment* and *requirements modeling.* It all made sense back then and certain aspects of the requirements-first/technology second adoption model still make sense today (which is why some companies still cling to the approach).

But things are different now: there are immediate business opportunities that emerging/disruptive technologies present to even the most conservative technology adopters, especially when the pressures to digitally transform organizations are at an all-time high.

Technology adoption today is unrelated to the so-called adoption *chasm* described by Geoffrey A. Moore (1991). Moore argued that there's a chasm between early adopters and the early majority that must be managed by high-tech marketers. The chasm is gone. Companies no longer even think in such terms: *our data suggest that technology is adopted as quickly as it arrives, and technology marketers are now almost always behind the technology adoption curve (though there are still some who insist on living in the twentieth century).*

Traditional technology adoption models were driven by detailed— and *validated*— requirements definitions. *But today's adoption models are often driven by requirements ignorance—heresy to many traditional technology buyers.* The approach assumes that technologies drive requirements—not the other way around—which is why many emerging technologies are *discovered* through deployment.

Marchand and Peppard (2013) make the same case regarding analytics projects. They describe what they call *discovery-driven project management* as comprised of the following steps:

1. Develop theories
2. Build hypotheses
3. Identify relevant data
4. Conduct experiments
5. Refine hypotheses in response to findings
6. Repeat the process

They argue that successful technology deployments are discovered *not managed*, and that companies should *experiment* with technologies until they find the right combination of requirements and technologies.

What about technology adoption and digital transformation?

By the way, what books, articles, or authors come to mind when managers and executives think about digital transformation? There are no *classics—yet*. A quick search will reveal books such as *e Digital Transformation Playbook* by David Rogers (2016) and papers and articles generated by consultancies such as McKinsey & Co. The lack of classics is not at all surprising given the relative newness of digital transformation as a formal strategic objective. In 10 or 20 years there will be books, articles, reports and cases that many of us will identify as transformative frameworks (though a lot of the Amazon *bestsellers* today will be discarded over time).

Emerging technology adoption can be transformative or just part of the *normal* digital transformation process. The keys are performance against a set of known *or-to-be-discovered* requirements, speed and cost: if you pilot, they will come.

The essence of ready organization, processes and governance is the formalization of immediate technology assessment and exploitation. The *rules* around all these are important especially because they define a company's technology culture. For many companies this represents a huge change in the way they see technology, in the way they track/acquire/pilot/deploy/assess/support technology, and how they define business agility. Learning how to immediately and seamlessly identify, pilot and deploy ready technologies is a skill that must be developed and institutionalized.

Why are things so different today than they were 5 or 10 years ago? There are at least five reasons (discussed throughout this book):

1. The pace of digital technology change has dramatically accelerated: fueled by Moore's Law, consumerization, globalization and a path to personal wealth creation that increasingly rewards technology entrepreneurs, digital technology is advancing at an unprecedented rate.
2. The cumulative impact of integrated technology solutions is rapidly expanding: integration and interoperability among technologies are rapidly growing, enabling rapid deployment through internally or externally enabled deployment; software architectures decreasingly require operation on but one device, operating system and the like: software now travels across networks and devices.
3. The ease of deploying emerging technologies out-of-the-gate is growing (principally through cloud delivery): rather than building data centers, deploying enterprise software applications and hiring huge teams, companies of all sizes can rapidly pilot and deploy emerging technologies with little or no initial cost via XaaS delivery models.
4. The cost of deploying emerging technologies has fallen significantly and shows every sign of falling even more through commoditization and increasingly favorable hardware and software price/performance ratios.
5. Companies understand that their ability to compete is tied directly to their ability to leverage digital technology generally and individual technologies specifically: the role that information technology plays in every aspect of business is increasing dramatically.

Our research may change your perspective on the technology adoption process and just how impactful emerging technology and technology delivery models can be. Said a little differently, our research results may inspire companies to commit requirements analysis heresy.

We collected data across multiple industries and countries, but primarily from the United States. There were nearly as many business professionals as technology professionals who responded to our survey. We also conducted numerous interviews with business and technology professionals.

The Cutter Consortium facilitated the data collection process. (The survey and interview questions appear in Appendices A and B.)

Very surprising were the extreme responses to survey questions about technology adoption: *nearly 70% of the companies do not have a defined process for adopting emerging/disruptive technologies.*

We were also surprised to learn that most companies—*nearly 70%*—have already gone to the *dark side adopting emerging technology without specific, validated requirements.*

The very idea that technologies would be acquired and deployed—however carefully or haphazardly—without documented, validated requirements flies in the face of what technology and business professionals were taught for decades in the twentieth century. In fact, it was often the *business* professionals who insisted on elaborate requirements gathering and validation prior to any technology purchases. Business professionals frequently complained about the rush-to-deploy untested technologies or—worse—technologies with unverified total-cost-of-ownership (TCO) or return-on-investment (ROI) calculi.

When we analyzed that thinking we discovered that nearly 70% of companies are very or somewhat comfortable with technology driving requirements versus the other way around.

These findings confirmed our core hypotheses (see below) about technology adoption: *companies are reacting to the pace of technology change, consumerization and the immediate need for digital transformation with completely new ways of thinking about how—and how quickly—to adopt emerging technology.*

In addition, the data told us something else about technology adoption: motivation. Why are companies even considering adopting new technology? *We discovered that fear, digital transformation and cost reduction are the major drivers of emerging/disruptive technology adoption.*

Given the *attitudes* about technology adoption—from both technology *and* business professionals—what emerging/disruptive technologies are in play? The *winners* include cloud computing, big data analytics, e-Learning, BYOD, mobile computing, wearables, location-based technologies, Internet-of-Things (IoT), e-Payment systems and digital security technologies, especially multilevel authentication.

These technologies were (and largely remain) on the 2016 and 2017 radar screens of large *and* small companies. These technologies made the list because they're *perceived* as the most potentially impactful along the continua of competitive fear, digital transformation and cost reduction—three stated reasons to pilot a suite of specific technologies.

Of special note is the variety of big data analytics planned pilots. Several years ago there was barely an understanding of structured versus unstructured data analytics, but today interest is strong in all kinds of analytics, reflecting a much deeper understanding of structured, unstructured, integrated, descriptive, explanatory, predictive and even prescriptive analytics.

Two unmistakable plans are clear: the intention to pilot multiple flavors of cloud computing and multiple big data analytics pilots. But what is surprising about this finding is not the general interest in cloud computing and analytics, but the *depth* of the interest in both. Companies have clearly distinguished among emerging and disruptive technologies within these broad technology families.

The data revealed some surprises, especially in corporate attitudes toward emerging/disruptive technology adoption and in overwhelming plans to pilot two classes of technologies—and the relative caution companies have in some forms of digital security and automated reasoning.

The results communicate several important attitudes, plans and trends about the adoption of emerging technology:

- Companies have thrown the old technology adoption models and processes out the window.
- The whole notion of *technology adoption categories*—such as innovators, early adopters, early majority, late majority and laggards—is obsolete: those who worried about *crossing the*

chasm appear to have no awareness of what that even means: the *chasm* is gone.

- Companies adopt technology because they are afraid, need to save money and want to digitally transform their tired business rules, processes and models, which explains why there's so much emphasis on digital transformation (fear and cost management are staples).
- *Shadow IT* spending *won* the spending war because it's no longer possible for enterprise IT to control technology spending primarily because cloud delivery has made it possible for business units to rapidly deploy and pilot emerging and disruptive technologies with no coordination with corporate or enterprise IT.
- Companies believe (2017) that there's platinum in analytics and cloud computing, gold in BYOD, wearables, e-Payment systems and e-Learning technologies but only silver in IoT and digital security.
- Companies are cautious about automated reasoning.
- Companies no longer have predominant technology development models such as the system development life cycle (SDLC), which they've replaced with a variety of development and deployment models with no names.
- Companies now have as many federated, decentralized and *other* governance structures as centralized ones—a major change from the twentieth century and after the effects of both the dot.com bust and great recession of 2008/2009.
- Companies are finally *professionalizing* emerging and disruptive technology adoption and creating variations of *innovation labs*. But it took them a long time to get there.
- Companies are rushing their pilots even if it means failing to measure success or failure: less than 30% even have return-on-investment measurement processes in place around their pilots.
- Due to the pace of technology change, fear, cost pressures and ongoing commitments to digital transformation, technology adoption will continue to occur at an increasing rate.
- Technology and business architecture consultants will exploit trends toward *technology-first-versus-requirements-second* emerging technology pilots.

- The health care and financial industries are leading the adoption of emerging/disruptive technologies, but over time nearly every vertical industry will ramp up their emerging/disruptive technology pilots.
- Rapid technology adoption will become a way of life in twenty-first century companies; the professionalization of technology adoption will increase dramatically over the next 5 years.

The data also suggest that these changes are well underway and the old ways of doing things are all but gone:

- The data suggest that the combination of digital velocity and transformation is tightly coupled and that the slow, careful and methodical adoption process will not enable meaningful transformation quickly enough for companies to stay competitive.
- Nothing is off-limits. Governance structures are changing. Adoption processes are changing. The list of technology targets is (constantly) changing.
- The companies that throw the old technology adoption and systems development methodologies playbooks out the window will win; those that insist on *discipline, process* and *repeatability* will lose.

The purpose of the research was to understand *how* companies identify, pilot and deploy specific emerging or disruptive digital technologies.

We asked the following questions:

- Are you still anchored in *requirements-first/technology-second* technology adoption processes? Why?
- What would happen if you threw the SDLC out the window—and just brought all kinds of new technologies into the company and started to pilot them?
- What examples do you have of successful and unsuccessful emerging technology pilots and deployments?
- In your view, are technologies/platforms/devices such as iPads, social media and analytics *ready to go*?
- What worries you about early/almost immediate technology adoption?

- How much Shadow IT is there at your company? Does Shadow IT fuel emerging technology adoption? Should you shut it down? Or should you let it go?
- What new/emerging/ready/disruptive technologies are high on your list? Which ones do you think have been overhyped?
- Do you think that the era of huge, proprietary platforms—such as enterprise resource planning (ERP), customer relationship management (CRM) and database management system (DBMS) platforms—is over? That it's now possible to integrate *pieces* of applications that used to be in a single platform through cloud SaaS providers?
- Do you think that *consumerization*—the adoption of emerging technology by consumers—has forever changed the business technology adoption process?

We received the following answers to these questions:

- Are you still anchored in *requirements-first/technology-second* technology adoption processes? Why?

  No—most companies have abandoned the requirements-first/ technology-second adoption process. Why? Because companies want to stay agile and competitive and want to transform their companies with digital technology.
- What would happen if you threw the SDLC out the window—and just brought all kinds of new technologies into the company and started to pilot them?

  Not much: the SDLC has already been replaced by other development models (such as Agile) and more importantly companies do not develop nearly as many applications as they did in the twentieth century.
- What examples do you have of successful and unsuccessful emerging technology pilots and deployments?

  Many: companies adopt emerging technologies, including devices, enterprise applications and especially mobile applications at an incredible pace. Failures are fast and inexpensive largely because of cloud delivery.
- In your view, are technologies/platforms/devices such as iPads, social media and analytics *ready to go*?

  Yes: easily ready for immediate pilots.

- What worries you about early/almost immediate technology adoption?

  Organizational roadblocks and outdated governance structures.

- How much Shadow IT is there at your company? Does Shadow IT fuel emerging technology adoption? Should you shut it down? Or should you let it go?

  Shadow IT has been with companies for decades. It's now an immediate adopter of emerging technology. Shadow IT should not disappear: it should be legalized.

- What new/emerging/disruptive technologies are high on your list? Which ones do you think have been overhyped?

  Cloud and analytics stand out; automated reasoning does not—yet.

- Do you think that the era of huge, proprietary platforms— such as ERP, CRM and DBMS platforms—is over? That it's now possible to integrate *pieces* of applications that used to be in a single platform through cloud SaaS providers?

  Cloud delivery of large enterprise software is keeping old, big platforms alive—for now; without cloud delivery, very few companies would embark on expensive, multiyear implementation big software projects.

- Do you think that *consumerization*—the adoption of emerging technology by consumers—has forever changed the business technology adoption process?

  Without question—and the trend will continue.

Our research suggests that emerging and disruptive technology is now perceived as a digital weapon. It is therefore often immediately piloted and quickly deployed by companies that want to improve their competitiveness through digital transformation. *We learned that digital transformation relies on the rapid adoption of emerging and sometimes disruptive technology.* (We also learned that digital transformation is a process that can be optimized in specific steps.)

Obviously *digital* transformation assumes the optimization of *digital technology*, but before companies cherry-pick technologies from pundit-pruned lists, they must conceptually understand what the technologies do and the degree of possible optimization-through-transformation. *In other words, digital transformation is most effective*

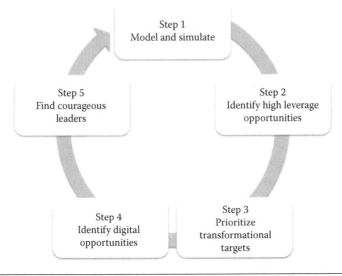

Figure ES.2　The digital transformation process.

when there is an objective and in which baskets of technologies are hypothetically linked to the objectives. This means that digital transformation is most effective when it's semifocused—which is a departure from the requirements-first/technology-second approach practiced in the twentieth century.

Figure ES.2 is the general roadmap that emerged from our data. Let's look at the five steps in some detail. Note that the steps comprise a framework, not a blueprint. Individual companies will architect their digital transformation projects according to their market positions, budgets and objectives (and even their corporate cultures).

- To initiate any transformation process, it's necessary to formally model corporate business processes and models with tools— such as business process modeling (BPM) and business architecture (BA) tools—that enable creative, empirical simulations.
- If companies cannot model their existing business processes and overall business models, they cannot transform their business.
- They should run the hypothetical models over and over again by changing the variables that predict to transformational outcomes.
- Modeling and simulation require subject matter expertise, discipline, tools and objectivity.

- Digital transformation requires some verifiable knowledge about the business rules, processes and models companies want to transform. This obviously requires domain expertise and the ability to model, simulate, test and transform impactful changes.
- Companies should identify leverage points in their business models and processes. Companies should do this by collecting data about the costs and benefits of the existing processes and models, and through *what–if* simulations of alternative improvements.
- Companies should also look at what their direct competitors are doing as well as companies in adjacent industries, but note that not every company, process, or business model will benefit from transformation.
- The outcome of this step in the transformation process is a list of high leverage opportunities for transformational change.
- Companies should prioritize transformation projects.
- Steps 1, 2 and 3 are about framing and anticipated leverage. They are necessary steps toward transformation and lead perfectly to the emerging technology adoption process.
- Companies should identify digital opportunities with the identification of emerging operational and strategic digital technologies and the roles they might play in the transformation process. This is precisely where technology adoption models scream.
- Companies committed to transformation are far more likely to pilot emerging technologies without requirements details. This is the essence of our emerging technology adoption findings.
- Once companies identify the emerging technologies that might enable the prioritized transformational projects, as part of the adoption process, they should simulate the current and expected technology capabilities with reference to the prioritized transformational functions.
- They should bet on a suite of transformational emerging and disruptive technologies: this step is the essence of what most professionals think digital transformation actually is, and most of them believe that digital transformation leverages emerging technologies.

- Successful digital transformation requires executive support. Remember, however, that the number of corporate executives, especially in cash-rich public companies, who really want to transform their companies, is relatively small. The opportunistic exception to this rule is where there's a strong correlation between the desire (D) for transformation and falling revenue and profits (FP), or $D + FP = DT$.
- Digital transformation and immediate emerging technology adoption are inseparable partners.

The inevitable conclusion is that digital transformation and rapid technology adoption are permanent partners. Neither of them can proceed without the other. Companies that must transform their business rules, processes and models—and this includes virtually every company on the planet—as well as companies that need to transform their technology infrastructures—must all track and pilot emerging and disruptive digital technologies as rapidly as possible. This is not the *innovator's dilemma*, but the *innovator's imperative*.

About the Authors

Stephen J. Andriole, PhD, is the Thomas G. Labrecque Professor of Business Technology at Villanova University, Villanova, Pennsylvania, where he teaches and conducts applied research in business technology management in the Villanova School of Business (VSB). He is formerly a professor of information systems and electrical and computer engineering at Drexel University, Philadelphia, Pennsylvania, and the George Mason Institute Professor and chairperson of the Department of Information Systems and Systems Engineering, George Mason University, Fairfax, Virginia. Dr. Andriole was the Director of the Cybernetics Technology Office of the Defense Advanced Research Projects Agency (DARPA). He was also the Chief Technology Officer and Senior Vice President of Safeguard Scientifics, Inc. and the Chief Technology Officer and Senior Vice President for technology strategy at Cigna Corporation. He is the founder and co-founder of several technology development and consulting companies and is an active Angel Investor in technology start-ups.

Some of his more than 30 books include *Applications in Artificial Intelligence* (Petrocelli Books, Inc., 1986), the *Sourcebook of Applied Artificial Intelligence* (McGraw-Hill, 1992), (coauthored with Len Adelman) a book on user interface technology for Lawrence Erlbaum Associates, Inc. titled *Cognitive Systems Engineering* (1995), a book for McGraw-Hill titled *Managing Systems Requirements: Methods, Tools & Cases* (1996), books on the *2nd Digital Revolution* (2005), *Technology Due Diligence* (2009)—for IGI Press—and *Best Practices in Business Technology Management* (2009), *IT's All About the People* (2011) for Auerbach Publications, and *Ready Technology: Fast Tracking New Business Technologies* (CRC Press, 2014).

He has published articles in the *Sloan Management Review, Software Development, IEEE Software, the Communications of the ACM, the Communications of the AIS, IEEE IT Professional and the Journal of Information Technology Research*, among other academic and practitioner journals. For more information about Dr. Andriole's research and publications please visit www.andriole.com.

Thomas Cox is a strategy consultant at AMR International, where he focuses on developing growth strategies and providing transactional support for multinational companies and investors. His project experience has included projects evaluating growth and entry options into the U.S. health care analytics market for a multinational data company, international expansion opportunities for a U.S. media and data company, and developing revenue growth strategies for a U.S. publishing company. He has also provided commercial due diligence for a variety of private equity firms. Prior to joining AMR, he worked as a business technology analyst at Deloitte Consulting LLP. He served as a research analyst for Villanova University's Center for Nonlinear Dynamics and Control (CENDAC), where he helped design and model an autonomous drone as part of Boeing-sponsored research initiative. He earned a BS in mechanical engineering from Villanova University.

Kaung M. Khin is a graduate student at Carnegie Mellon University, Pittsburgh, Pennsylvania, where he studies information systems with a concentration on business intelligence and data analytics. He worked in a real estate fund where he supported the fund's pursuit of acquisition, investment and loan opportunities by engaging in sophisticated financial modeling, due diligence and research. He also worked at a private equity firm with a focus on analytics and the health care industries. He graduated from Villanova University with a BBA in finance and management information systems, with a minor in business analytics.

1

TECHNOLOGY ADOPTION AND DIGITAL TRANSFORMATION

The results reported in this book are based on 5 years of research conducted at the Villanova School of Business, University in Villanova, Pennsylvania. The overarching hypothesis was that companies no longer adopt technology in any sort of phased way and the days when anyone worried about *crossing the chasm* are long gone. We also learned that digital transformation and rapid technology adoption are perfect partners.

We learned that companies have abandoned their obsession with *requirements* and have endorsed a *technology-first/requirements-second* approach to technology adoption. We learned that companies focused on digital transformation often adopt emerging technologies immediately. We learned that technology is driving business strategy and that companies are rethinking and reorganizing their technology organizations, especially the governance that determines how and why technology investments are made.

Phase 1 of the research was conceptual and described in *Ready Technology: Fast Tracking New Business Technologies* (Andriole, 2014a). The concept was simple: companies no longer conduct elaborate requirement analyses as part of the technology adoption process. Instead, companies immediately pilot and deploy emerging technologies without knowing exactly what problems the technologies might solve.

Phase 2 of the research involved collecting data about the technology adoption process to test the hypotheses generated in Phase 1.

They too were confirmed.

Here's what the data revealed:

- Companies have thrown the old technology adoption models and processes out the window.
- The whole notion of *technology adoption categories*—such as innovators, early adopters, early majority, late majority, and laggards—is obsolete: those who worried about *crossing the chasm* appear to have no knowledge of what that even means.
- Companies adopt technology because they are afraid of the competition, need to save money and want to digitally transform their tired business rules, processes and models, which explain why there's so much emphasis on digital transformation.
- *Shadow IT* spending *won* the spending war because it's no longer possible for enterprise *IT* to control technology spending—because cloud delivery has made it possible for business units to rapidly deploy and pilot emerging and disruptive technologies independently with no coordination with corporate or enterprise IT.
- Companies believe (in 2017) that there's platinum in analytics and cloud computing, gold in BYOD, wearables, e-Payment systems and e-Learning technologies but only silver in Internet-of-Things (IoT) and digital security.
- Companies are cautious about automated reasoning.
- Companies no longer embrace predominant technology development models similar to the system development life cycle (SDLC), which they've replaced with a variety of development and deployment models with no names.
- Companies now have as many federated, decentralized and *other* governance structures as centralized ones—a major change from the twentieth century and after the effects of both the dot.com bust and great recession of 2008/2009.
- Companies are finally *professionalizing* emerging/disruptive technology adoption and creating formal innovation labs, though it took them a long time to get there.
- Companies are rushing their pilots even if it means failing to measure success or failure: less than 30% even have return-on-investment measurement processes in place around their pilots.

- Due to the pace of technology change, fear, cost pressures and on-going commitments to digital transformation, technology adoption will continue to occur at an increasing rate.
- Technology and business architecture consultants will exploit trends toward *technology-first versus requirements-second* emerging technology pilots.
- The health care and financial industries are leading the adoption of emerging/disruptive technologies, but over time nearly every vertical industry increases the number of emerging/disruptive technology pilots.
- Rapid technology adoption will become a way of life for twenty-first century companies; the professionalization of technology adoption will increase dramatically over the next 5 years.

The following data also suggest that these changes are well underway and the old ways of doing things are all but gone:

- The data suggest that the combination of digital velocity and transformation are tightly coupled and that the slow, careful and methodical adoption process will not enable meaningful transformation quickly enough for companies to stay competitive.
- Nothing is off-limits. Governance structures are changing. Adoption processes are changing. The list of technology targets is (constantly) changing.
- The companies that throw the old technology adoption and systems development methodologies playbooks out the window will win; those that insist on requirements *discipline, process, standardization, validation* and *repeatability* will lose.

The purpose of this research was to understand *how* companies identify, pilot and deploy specific emerging or disruptive digital technologies.

We asked the following questions:

- Are you still anchored in *requirements-first/technology-second* technology adoption processes? Why?
- What would happen if you threw the SDLC out the window—and just brought all kinds of new technologies into the company and started to pilot them?

- What examples do you have of successful and unsuccessful emerging technology pilots and deployments?
- In your view, are technologies/platforms/devices such as iPads, social media and analytics *ready to go*?
- What worries you about early/almost immediate technology adoption?
- How much Shadow IT is there at your company? Does Shadow IT fuel emerging technology adoption? Should you shut it down? Or should you let it go?
- What new/emerging/ready/disruptive technologies are high on your list? Which ones do you think have been overhyped?
- Do you think that the era of huge, proprietary platforms—such as ERP, CRM and DBMS platforms—is over? That it's now possible to integrate *pieces* of applications that used to be in a single platform through cloud SaaS providers?
- Do you think that *consumerization*—the adoption of emerging technology by consumers—has forever changed the business technology adoption process?

We received the following answers to these questions:

- Are you still anchored in *requirements-first/technology-second* technology adoption processes? Why?
  No—most companies have abandoned the requirements-first/ technology-second adoption process. Why? Because companies want to stay agile and competitive, and want to transform their companies with digital technology.
- What would happen if you threw the SDLC out the window—and just brought all kinds of new technologies into the company and started to pilot them?
  Not much: The SDLC has already been replaced by other develop- ment models (such as Agile) and more importantly companies do not develop nearly as many applications as they did in the twentieth century.
- What examples do you have of successful and unsuccessful emerging technology pilots and deployments?

Many: Companies adopt emerging technologies including devices, enterprise applications and especially mobile applications at an incredible pace. Failures are fast and inexpensive largely because of cloud delivery.

- In your view, are technologies/platforms/devices such as iPads, social media and analytics *ready to go?*
Yes: Easily ready for immediate pilots.

- What worries you about early/almost immediate technology adoption?
Organizational roadblocks and outdated governance structures.

- How much Shadow IT is there at your company? Does Shadow IT fuel emerging technology adoption? Should you shut it down? Or should you let it go?
Shadow IT has been with companies for decades. It's now an immediate adopter of emerging technology. Shadow IT should not disappear: it should be legalized.

- What new/emerging/disruptive technologies are high on your list? Which ones do you think have been overhyped?
Cloud and analytics stand out; automated reasoning does not—yet.

- Do you think that the era of huge, proprietary platforms— such as ERP, CRM and DBMS platforms—is over? That it's now possible to integrate *pieces* of applications that used to be in a single platform through cloud SaaS providers?
Cloud delivery of large enterprise software is keeping old and big platforms alive—for now; without cloud delivery, very few companies would embark on expensive, multiyear implementation of big software projects.

- Do you think that *consumerization*—the adoption of emerging technology by consumers—has forever changed the business technology adoption process?
Without question—and the trend will continue.

Our research suggests that emerging technology is now perceived as a digital weapon and therefore must be immediately piloted and then deployed by companies that want to improve their competitiveness through digital transformation.

Emerging Technology and Digital Transformation

The most important driver of immediate technology adoption is the commitment many companies make to digital transformation. Every board of directors and senior management team aspire to the efficiencies and competitiveness that digital transformation might deliver. But the path to transformation—as we all learned in the 1990s when *business process reengineering* was all the rage—is mined with explosives. Digital transformation, similar to all major corporate initiatives, must be well planned and exquisitely executed.

Everyone wants to transform their business, *and everyone knows that transformation primarily depends on leveraging the right digital technology at the right time on the right processes at the right cost* (Andal-Ancion et al., 2003; Agarwal et al., 2010; Lucas, 2014).

But what *is* digital transformation?

Jason Bloomberg (2014) talks about digital transformation *ignorance* in no uncertain terms:

> Altimeter Group released their new report on The 2014 State of Digital Transformation by Brian Solis earlier this week. The central conclusion of the report, which is available for free download: only one-quarter of the companies we surveyed have a clear understanding of new and under-performing digital touchpoints, yet 88% of the same cohort reports that they are undergoing digital transformation efforts. In other words, the vast majority of people Altimeter interviewed for this report claimed they are undergoing Digital Transformation, even though most of them don't know what it is.

According to Wikipedia (2016), let's think about digital transformation like this:

> Digital transformation refers to the changes associated with the application of digital technology in all aspects of human society. Digital transformation may be thought as the third stage of embracing digital technologies: digital competence → digital literacy → digital transformation. The latter stage means that digital usages inherently enable new types of innovation and creativity in a particular domain, rather than simply enhance and support the traditional methods. Digital

transformation affects both individual businesses and whole segments of the society, such as government, mass communications, art, medicine or science.

With all this in mind, there are at least five steps to successful digital transformation. The steps are based on the data we collected at the Cutter Consortium and Villanova University. The steps also dovetail with the results of our technology adoption research.

Note that the best practices described here do not begin with long lists of emerging technologies that everyone's talking about, as potentially disruptive as they might be. Obviously *digital* transformation assumes the optimization of *digital technology*, but before companies cherry-pick technologies from pundit-pruned lists, they must conceptually understand what the technologies do, how they do, what they do and the degree of possible optimization-through-transformation—regardless of the transformation approach. *In other words, digital transformation is most effective when there's an objective and in which baskets of technologies are linked to the objectives. This means that digital transformation is most effective when it's at least semi-focused.*

Figure 1.1 shows the general roadmap that emerged from the data. Let's look at the five steps in some detail. Note that the steps comprise

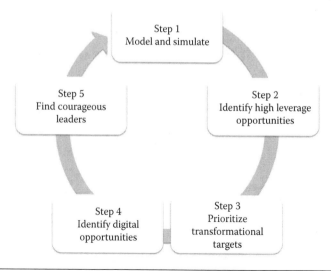

Figure 1.1 The digital transformation process.

a framework, not a blueprint. Individual companies will architect their digital transformation projects according to their market positions, budgets and objectives.

Step 1: Model and Simulate

To initiate any transformation process, it's necessary to formally model corporate business processes and models with tools—such as business process modeling (BPM) and business architecture (BA) tools—that enable creative, empirical simulations. If companies cannot model their existing business processes and overall business models, they cannot transform their business. To map processes *objectively*, companies should use external vertical industry consultants to model the processes and invite internal subject matter experts (SMEs) to participate in the development of transformation hypotheses. They should run the hypothetical models over and over again by changing the variables that predict to transformational outcomes.

Modeling and simulation require SME, discipline, tools *and objectivity*, which is why external consultants are often best suited to modeling and simulation. The models are the infrastructure on which digital transformation is built. If the infrastructure is weak, the digital transformation process will collapse.

BPM/BA efforts can also be expensive, time-consuming and iterative, so companies should not expect transformation results overnight, or even a transformation plan, until all of their business processes are identified, described, cataloged and simulated. If the digital transformation and senior management teams are unwilling or are unable to accept the size and persistence of digital transformation investments, digital transformation initiatives should not be launched.

The message here is that digital transformation requires some verifiable knowledge about the business rules, processes and models companies want to transform. This obviously requires domain expertise and the ability to model, simulate, test and transform impactful changes.

Step 2: Identify High-Leverage Opportunities

Some corporate processes are broken. Managers and executives have known about them for years. But the cost/benefit calculations around replacement have always been challenging. So nothing changes. But following a serious, formal BPM process followed by simulations of alternative processes, there's an opportunity to identify the processes likely to have greatest transformational impact. This should be the outcome of Step 2.

Companies should identify these leverage points in their business models and processes. Companies should do this by collecting data about the costs and benefits of the existing processes and models, and through *what-if* simulations of alternative improvements.

Companies should also look at what their direct competitors are doing as well as companies in adjacent industries. If simulation results fall short of measurable meaningful transformation, they should stop testing. *More heresy: not every company, process or business model will benefit from transformation.*

The outcome of this step in the transformation process is a list of high-leverage opportunities for transformational change. Since this list will be *political*, companies should use as many outsiders as possible to develop the initial list.

Here are some examples:

- We need to transform the sales process
- We need to improve innovation
- We need to improve quality
- We need to up-sell and cross-sell more effectively
- We need to develop new products and services

Step 3: Prioritize Transformation Targets

From the options list, companies should prioritize transformation projects. This step is complicated because it's the first one to address resource constraints. Some opportunities will not be pursued. Others will be placed on hold. The result of the exercise will be a short list of transformation targets.

Steps 1, 2 and 3 are about framing and anticipated leverage. They are necessary steps toward transformation and lead perfectly to the emerging technology adoption process.

Let's highlight Steps 1, 2 and 3 of the digital transformation process. We do this here because of the importance of executing these steps with care.

Careful Modeling   Process modeling is organizationally challenging. Yes, there are powerful methods and tools to assist you. There are experienced consultants who will work with you, and there are sincere (and insincere) internal champions of modeling efforts.

But there are political landmines everywhere.

Begin the modeling process with a *consensus test*, which identifies process areas—such as supply chain or inventory management—in which there's relative consensus about inefficiencies. CRM could be another area, or even billing. Do not model processes that are measurably *OK*, or processes that the competition is modeling unless their problems are also your problems.

Next, measure the internal *embarrassment quotient*. Who will be embarrassed by the results of the consensus test? Relative consensus about failed or broken processes notwithstanding, when a process is listed as *officially* failed or broken—and therefore the target of formal modeling—someone will be embarrassed. Make sure that any reputational damage to individuals and teams is managed and make sure that *accountability* is not used as a weapon to crush political enemies: be extremely careful if the broken process belongs to a member of the senior management team.

One way to accomplish this *part* of this goal is to emphasize the *quantitative-empirical over the qualitative-subjective. The data is the data* is a good phrase to repeat while always avoiding phrases such as, *it's all Tom's fault*! But regardless of how hard you try to avoid innuendos and implications, Tom may still get blamed for making the transformational list. You have to deal with Tom—and his enemies (that you're modeling work has empowered).

Another way to accomplish the modeling goal is to *emphasize SME*: make sure that the modeling team is substantively credible beyond reproach. This is not the time to hire horizontal consultants who are fresh out of graduate school to lecture the team on *Porter's 5 Forces*. Instead, hire consultants with deep experience in your vertical industry who can hold their own with longstanding, well-respected industry veterans—*and anyone in your company who claims to know it all*.

Begin the modeling process with simple models about which there is relatively little disagreement. For example, begin the BPM process with straightforward *descriptive* models of the processes in question, such as inventory management, CRM, sales or marketing. These *descriptive* models should be industry-validated *before* turning to the *prescriptive* models intended to improve the failed/broken processes under scrutiny. Although it will be challenging to forge agreement about how current processes actually work, it will be much more difficult to achieve consensus about how the failed/broken process should be remodeled: *the pivot from descriptive to prescriptive modeling is the most challenging part of the BPM process. Anticipate it, manage it and optimize it—or the whole BPM exercise will collapse.*

Tools are always important. There are many tools out there that will do the job. Make sure you select a tool that enables quick answers to *what if* questions and one that empirically describes, explains and prescribes outcomes. Do not select an overly complicated tool with features that will never be used, and make sure the displays these tools generate are easily comprehensible to BPM novices. If someone says, *I have no idea what this display is telling me,* find another tool.

Leveraging → Prioritization   As we said:

> Following a serious, formal BPM process followed by detailed simulations of alternative processes, there's an opportunity to identify—with empirical evidence—the processes likely to have greatest transformational impact ... do this by collecting empirical data about the costs and benefits of the existing processes and models, and through "what-if" simulations of alternative improvements ... (but) if simulation results fall short of measurable meaningful transformation, stop testing: not every company, process or business model will benefit from transformation.

Forging consensus about which processes are failing or broken and which improved ones can generate the greatest impact requires every soft skill you can find. But it also requires as much real data as possible. This is the middle ground that every transformation manager must find. But at the end of the day, the prioritization process is political, though informed—*but not decided*—by BPM data.

We remember well a large BPM project implemented at Shire Pharmaceuticals. There was initial consensus about the approach and ultimate value of BPM, but when the results were released there was nothing short of disinterest among the stakeholders. The modeled processes were absolutely *broken* but not so much as to threaten the company's primary revenue stream. Even the leader of the business unit processes most in need of *transformation* supported the BPM project through a series of politically correct interviews and round-tables. Everyone was excited that the process owner was participating personally in the effort to improve *her* processes! Her agreeing that *her* processes were absolutely broken did not necessarily mean she intended to make major changes. She happily participated because she understood that improving even broken processes would have little impact on the price of the stock, the size of executive bonuses or the long-term viability of the business. So rather than upset any apple carts, she punted.

So what to do?

Start small by gathering as much support as possible. Make sure that everyone keeps the transformational goal in sight. As we said:

> Is it to save money, increase market share, increase profitability, retain employees, disrupt a company and industry … what? You must know where you're going to get there. You also need to reality check your prioritized objectives according to budget, time, talent and market constraints: use outside consultants who have no vested financial interests in their recommendations to screen transformation alternatives. Never rely on internal professionals to adopt or reject transformational options. Their recommendations will be influenced by too many vested human and financial interests. From the options list, identify and integrate specific transformation projects to be led by outsiders: insiders may sabotage transformation processes.

Said differently, find a savvy HR professional, a psychiatrist and maybe even a soothsayer to help you manage the BPM process. Watch for landmines and backstabbers while you find and value legitimate partners. Emphasize wherever and whenever you can *the quantitative-empirical results* of your BPM analyses.

Keep IT Real You still need to match all this with the right digital technologies and find senior leadership that will stay with your BPM projects before, during and after good *and* bad results. As we've said:

> The number of corporate executives, especially in public companies, who really want to transform their companies is relatively small. The major

exception to this rule is the strong correlation between the desire (D) for transformation and falling revenue and profits (FP), or $D + FP = DT$. Digital transformation … is slow and iterative: industries do not transform themselves overnight.

Steps 1, 2 and 3 of the transformation process must be implemented carefully and thoughtfully. Failure in the beginning will result in failure at the end.

Step 4: Identify Digital Opportunities

This step begins with the identification of emerging operational and strategic digital technologies and the roles they might play in the transformation process. *This is precisely where technology adoption models scream.* When business process reengineering was all the rage in the twentieth century, companies developed detailed requirement models of specific processes they were trying to improve. The devil was definitely in the details, which often undermined serious reengineering projects. *Today, companies committed to transformation are far more likely to pilot emerging technologies without requirement details. This is the essence of our emerging technology adoption findings.*

Once companies identify the emerging technologies that might enable the prioritized transformational projects, as part of the adoption process, they should simulate the current and expected technology capabilities with reference to the prioritized transformational functions. Companies should find the smartest consultants they can find to describe future technology capabilities. They should bet on a suite of transformational emerging technologies. Step 4 is the essence of what most professionals think digital transformation actually is, and most of them believe that digital transformation leverages emerging technologies.

A great deal of transformational leverage still comes from operational and strategic technology rather than from emerging technology. This is because many business models and processes are antiquated, as evidenced by the relative ease with which, for example, *Uber* replaced taxis and *Airbnb* replaced hotels. Of course, there are countless ways through which emerging technology can improve—and even disrupt—processes and even whole industries, but real leverage often lies with emerging technology.

Does this mean that there is no possibility for true *disruption*? No, it does not, but it does mean that true disruption is less likely to occur in established companies with consistent revenue streams. Emerging and especially disruptive technologies are used by start-ups to disrupt well-established markets. The reasons for this trend are many, but suffice it to say that established companies are *established* because they've reached some level of revenue generation driven by relatively well-understood processes that together comprise an ongoing business model. They are therefore unwilling to disrupt much of anything. Start-ups, on the other hand, are completely unencumbered by revenue streams—*usually because they have no revenue.* Their mission is to invent, so they're much more likely to disrupt old processes and models or create whole new ones with emerging and truly disruptive digital technology. *Similarly, early stage and midsized companies—and larger companies with sputtering business models—will pursue transformation through the immediate adoption of emerging and hopefully disruptive technology* (Andriole, 2017a).

Step 5: Find Courageous Leaders

The search for courageous leaders could easily have been the first step in the digital transformation process. One could argue that without courageous leadership it makes no sense to take any steps at all. At the same time, the business case for digital transformation—and emerging technology adoption—is generally what leaders need to see before they agree to support a serious transformation initiative. So, the search for courageous leaders could certainly begin before, during or after transformational program planning.

The number of corporate executives, especially in cash-rich public companies, who really want to transform their companies, is relatively small. The major exception to this rule is where there's a strong correlation between the desire (D) for transformation and *falling* revenue and profits (FP), or D + FP = DT.

The whole idea of *disruption* is an external abstraction: how many companies have we seen that have—*without market duress*—successfully transformed their business models? Change is expensive, time-consuming, inexact and painful. It's also a political target: despite what best-selling business books and *pundits speaking for huge lunch time fees* tell us, most human beings despise change, which means that transformation is constrained. The most grandiose disruptive digital transformation (D²T) will likely come from start-ups and failing, vertically *established* companies. Grandiose *corporate* transformation is as unlikely as grandiose *industry* transformation is likely.

There's a nagging requirement to disrupt everything all the time, if only *Blockbuster* had become *Netflix* and *Borders* had become *Amazon*. Digital transformation is slow and iterative: industries do not transform themselves overnight. *Facebook* was founded in 2004, *Airbnb* was founded in 2008, and *Uber* was founded in 2009. (Whole industries are seldom transformed by established market leaders either.)

Step 5 of the process is the key to successful digital transformation. It's also where immediate emerging and potentially disruptive technology adoption occurs.

Digital transformation and immediate emerging technology adoption are inseparable partners. Our findings are interesting as standalone insights into the technology adoption process, but they're much more important to the success—or failure—of the digital transformation process. Hopefully, the research described here will inspire more—*and more aggressive*—digital transformation.

One more thing: successful technology adopters and digital transformers *speak digital*.

Digital is a new language. *Information Technology* (*IT*) was an old, difficult language that no one actually spoke except around data centers and help desks. It was confined to technologists who lived and breathed bits, bytes and lights. Every so often the technologists were required to speak to their bosses (and their bosses' bosses) about technology. We've given—and witnessed—many of these *briefings* in which most of the briefing content flew right over the heads of *management*. Depending on the briefer, some of it generated hostility from managers and executives who felt that the technologists were arrogant, condescending and, worst of all, incomprehensible.

Back in the twentieth century, management was at a comprehension disadvantage: it literally had no idea what their techies were saying about server farms, data extraction, transformation and loading (ETL) or help desk ticketing. So, they nodded as though they understood what the techie was saying. But the language was as baffling as the nodding.

Digital is different. It's quickly becoming a universal language. This is because of the following reasons: (1) technology has consumerized, because (2) technology is now covered extensively by the popular media and (3) because managers and executives increasingly came of leadership age with PCs, cell phones and e-mail. *The techie who thinks he or she can deceive an executive about business technology with deliberately obtuse language should be coached in another direction.*

So, how should technologists speak *digital?* There are five steps that can help:

Profile the Audience   First, technologists should profile their managers and executives to determine how just wide and deep their digital knowledge is. Some managers are near-techies themselves. They have their own personal technology infrastructures: their own *Dropbox* accounts, multiple e-mail accounts and *Twitter*, and *Facebook* and *Instagram* accounts. Everyone has a *LinkedIn* profile, a smartphone and a tablet. *Fewer and fewer managers and executives actually use PCs, because they can manage their personal and professional lives with other tools.* These managers and executives are technologically savvy and more than that capable of holding their own in conversations about mobility, infrastructure and cloud delivery. Although they may not be able to debate strengths/weaknesses/oppurtunities/threats (SWOTs) around alternative cloud architectures, they usually fully understand the concepts around cloud hosting, multilevel authentication, social media and mobility, among other key digital concepts, tools and processes. On the other hand, there are managers and executives that are only *users* of technology and have limited knowledge of how anything really works. Speaking digital to each type is different—not to form, but to content: users need more information than aficionados. *But unlike in the twentieth century, digital technologists can build on a generalized technology knowledge base that accelerates its understanding.* It's important to always realize that managers and executives grew up with technology.

Stick to the Business   Digital technologists should only talk about technology in the context of business models, processes and problems: digital is a vitamin pill, and should be described as such. Twentieth century technologists spoke about technology as painkillers that had to be tightly managed. These were unhappy discussions that everyone dreaded and often ended with some executive complaining about the cost of technology *and not what technology could do for the business.* Digital technology is a business solution, not a problem, and should be presented that way. Digital technologies that fall into the pain-killer-versus-vitamin-pill trap will quickly discover just how skeptical some (especially older) executives can be about the cost-versus-benefit of digital technology—even today. Digital technologists should also appreciate the importance of bottom lines. Business managers and executives need to understand how digital technology will help or hurt the business not just in terms of costs versus business benefits, but also in terms of risks. Note that managers and executives are now keenly interested in digital security because breaches threaten their companies and their careers. Speaking about digital requires a new interpretation of traditional SWOT analyses.

Executives also crave information about so-called disruptive technologies, especially the ones their rivals are deploying. *Digital technologists should be executive spies. They should be business consultants with deep industry domain expertise. They should be digital saviors.*

Clarity—at 500 Feet Unlike IT, *digital* technology requires relatively little precision. Since we've moved to cloud delivery, we no longer need to know who made the servers that host our applications or how often they need to be replaced. Such details are meaningless today. Twentieth century techies were obsessed with server vendors, maintenance, backup and recovery; no one cares about such things when digital transformation is a business goal.

Speaking digital is purposeful dialog focused on business processes and objectives. Fortunately, this means that deploying a new application no longer requires long discussions about software development methodologies or whether the programmers can handle requirements, especially when they're offshore. Debates about cloud security are appropriate and necessary, but should be more about industry *compliance* than security *technology*. Cloud delivery has forever changed the nature and level of technology conversations because the cloud itself provides the technological plumbing necessary to enable and optimize business processes. Although we agonized in the twentieth century about plumbers and plumbing, today we can focus on business architects and strategists without the drag of leaking pipes. *Speaking digital is all about speaking strategically.*

Consistent, Relevant, Templated Agenda Digital technologists should focus on new technology, new technology delivery and the strategic role that technology can play in competitiveness and profitability. The discussion agenda should align with all this by identifying macro and disruptive technology trends. Although the list will change over time, there is a set of technology opportunities that should be on every digital technologist's communications list. Think of them as talking points:

- Business processes and business models
- Disruptive technologies
- Competitor technology pilots
- Business agility
- Cloud delivery
- Digital security

Managers and executives should hear about these areas every time digital technologists brief them.

Partners, Never Students Digital technologists should never lecture. Lecturing is something that twentieth century technologists often did to educate technologically ignorant managers and executives. It was fun to feel superior, though it usually backfired. Speaking digital is about communication with partners, never with students, and because all communication is relationship-based, digital technologists should develop as many relationships as possible across the organizations, especially with colleagues throughout the business. This requires technologists to become highly credible SMEs. It also requires them to demonstrate real empathy for the competitive and profitability pressures that business professionals experience every single day. Conversations about digital technology should never be framed around *listen to me, let me tell you how all this works*, or *leave it to me*. Instead, the conversation should be framed around *let's solve this* and *let's see if this technology helps you increase market share*. As *technology* has ascended to the cloud anyway, it's now time to speak a language that assumes purpose and outcomes.

A Growing Threat

There's a growing threat lurking around all digital transformation projects and especially the rapid adoption of emerging and disruptive technology. It's important for all business technologists to appreciate the nature of the threat before they embark on any transformation projects with any kind of technology. The reference here is to the digital crime wave that's already on us.

Look at the following technology trends:

1. Cryptocurrency
2. Cloud delivery
3. Self-driving cars, planes and ships
4. Military, industrial and personal drones
5. Medical wearables
6. Personal and professional robots
7. Digital home automation
8. Networked devices via the Internet-of-Things (IoT)
9. Location-based services
10. Automated reasoning
11. Digitally managed digital infrastructures
12. Digitally managed physical infrastructures
13. Robotic surgery
14. Augmented reality
15. 3D printing

If we were all cyber criminals, we'd be giddy. Although ransomware is a rising threat, it's child's play compared to what's coming. Hollywood screenwriters are overwhelmed with possibilities. Novelists are exhausted with plots. Social media is already describing scenarios of digital death, doom and destruction. So, what *is* the state of risk that the industry is creating? The cumulative effect is positively frightening.

There are significant profiles of each of the above trends. Hacking implanted medical devices such as pacemakers and insulin pumps have been analyzed. Johnson & Johnson recently warned its customers about the risks around their insulin pumps. According to Jim Hinkle (2016) reporting in Reuters this past October:

> Johnson & Johnson is telling patients that it has learned of a security vulnerability in one of its insulin pumps that a hacker could exploit to overdose diabetic patients with insulin, though it describes the risk as low.

Pacemakers can be hacked; electronic medical records can be hacked; robotic surgeons can be hacked.

We could cite similar risks in each of the aforementioned 15 areas. We could easily increase the number of targets and risks. We all can imagine countless threat/risk scenarios. Some of them are just annoying but many are disastrous.

We can be confident that the number, nature and severity of cybercrimes will dramatically increase. We can also be confident that criminal creativity will boggle our minds and that we will look at simple credit card number theft as Cybercrime 101. We will see the rise of digitally organized crime and the need for as many digital cops as there are cops on the street. We will see countries increase their digital military budgets while reducing their budgets for tanks and fighter aircraft: dueling intelligent machines will fight wars. If you think all this is science fiction, focus on the aforementioned list of 15 areas and the digital science around all this—and then check your insulin pump, your pacemaker, your home HVAC system, your car, your surgeon and, of course, your credit card and passwords. The number of local, regional and global cyber detectives will explode—as will cybercrime budgets. The legal system will play continuous catch-up to deal with what cybercriminals do.

Everyone is now taking Cybercrime 101. The good guys will learn about risks and risk mitigation. But the bad guys will learn about vulnerabilities, tools and methods. It's like sending the world to a gun safety course and expecting everyone to only learn about safety while promising to never use guns to do anything wrong. A digital crime wave is coming and it's coming fast. Watch the companies most vulnerable to the digital crime wave and the companies that respond to digital crimes. They will have to be smarter and faster than the cybercriminals. Are they up to the task? Will the government under- or overregulate? Will insurance companies come to the rescue? Will Internet providers cleanse their pipes? Will the FBI help? Will the military play a role?

It's important for us to acknowledge the nature and depth of the threat that surrounds the adoption of all technologies, especially emerging and disruptive technology.

Digital transformation with emerging and disruptive technology can occur faster with rapid technology adoption. But it can also hemorrhage. Sometimes the risks are organic and sometimes the risks are created by outside parties. Cybersecurity risks cannot be separated from technology adoption or the digital transformation it enables.

Although it may be disheartening to end this chapter on a threatening note, it's essential we appreciate the breadth and depth of the threat to our digital infrastructures and applications. Rapid technology adoption and digital transformation can—and will—proceed, but we must understand that the success of these efforts increases personal and professional digital security risks. These concerns should provide context to rapid technology adoption and digital transformation—just like the list of side effects that pharmaceutical companies are required to disclose about their drugs.

2

Phased Technology Adoption in the Twentieth Century

The *New York Times* reported in 2011 that 93% of the *Fortune 500* companies began testing and deploying *iPads* shortly after their initial release to the public. The *Times* concluded that the immediate adoption of *iPads* was due to the *consumerization* of technology. By making technology different and fun, Apple won the hearts and wallets of consumers *and* managers.

Was *iPad* adoption an anomaly or a precursor of technology adoption trends?

The time from market availability to market penetration of the largest technological innovations of the past century is shrinking. As technologies become better, faster, cheaper and *easier*, the rate of adoption accelerates. In fact, if we look at the adoption rates of telephones, televisions, air travel and refrigerators versus the adoption rates of video games, credit cards, social media and computer tablets, we see that rates sometimes spread over decades versus rates that spread over years—or even months.

Our research around technology adoption examined the governing theories behind technology adoption and even how vendors try to forecast the sales and adoption rates of new technologies. We looked at popular theories and frameworks that influence how technologies ultimately penetrate the enterprise. We looked at historical technology adoption processes and why phased adoption approaches were so popular for so long.

We also examined technology adoption in the twentieth century using *Crossing the Chasm*, *The Innovator's Dilemma*, and the *diffusion of innovations* approaches to technology adoption as focal points.

Traditional Technology Adoption Models

We examined the following three most cited models:

1. Bass diffusion model—Frank Bass (1969)
2. Hype cycle—Vedrashko (2008)
3. Diffusion of innovations—Everett Rogers (1962)

We asked the following questions about the models:

1. How widely used is the model today?
2. How useful is the model today?
3. What assumptions does the model make that are now invalid?

Although these models are still in use, the assumptions around their relevance are no longer valid and, worse, could lead companies to competitive disadvantage.

The Bass Diffusion Model

Predictive modeling is highly valued by financial institutions and corporate strategists.

It's a highly iterative process that requires deep knowledge of the drivers, levers and external factors (independent variables) to get an accurate prediction of events (dependent variables). But what makes modeling harder today than it was 10 or 20 years ago is the amount of statistical entropy in our personal and professional lives (which is partly why so many *Wall Street* traders were unable to forecast the great recession of 2008/2009 and why statistical pollsters failed to predict the outcome of the 2016 U.S. presidential election).

This was not always the case. Historically, modeling technology adoption rates were simpler because there were fewer confounding variables. The oft-discussed adoption rate of air conditioners during the period from 1947 to 1961 is a case in point where predicted and actual adoption rates easily converged (Bass, 1969). Using the Bass diffusion model, vendors of air conditioners could determine the timing and magnitude of peak sales. The same could also be done with television sets, cell phones and other early electronics. The model was particularly accurate in modeling the adoption rates of durable goods such as clothes dryers and steam irons.

The model's founder, Frank Bass, created the differential equation under the assumption that *the rate of adoption of a new product depends on the degree of innovativeness and imitation among adopters,* that is, how unique the product was, and the more widely talked about and replicated by consumers and competitive companies, the better the model worked. This concept of imitation parallels our hypothesis that consumerization is a strong driver of technology adoption. Frank Bass's model has been updated and refined mathematically several times, since its initial publication in 1963, but still maintains its foundational concepts.

But the Bass model's accuracy and precision exhibited in the mid- to late twentieth century is much less accurate today. This is because of the model's inherent limitations that were further compounded by the complexities of today's emerging and disruptive technologies because of the following reasons:

1. The model's coefficients can be often under- and overestimated by 20%–30%, leading to significant inaccuracies (Van den Bulte and Lilien, 1997).
2. The model does not include the direct influence of any marketing variables such as price or advertising that are often used as levers by technology vendors.
3. The model is static and assumes that the product itself doesn't change over time.
4. The model is limited in its predictive use cases as the model requires as inputs two most important events that managers would like to predict: takeoff and slowdown (Chandrasekaran and Tellis, 2007)

With today's pace of technology adoption and deployment, these inaccuracies and limitations would be costly and potentially dangerous to any technology vendor trying to forecast sales. In fact, there are numerous examples of emerging technology adoptions that illustrate the following points:

- Massive growth in music streaming when users decided that Spotify's freemium pricing model was more attractive than paying 99 cents per song on iTunes.

- The success in any start-up that invests heavily in advertising over product development (e.g., Rocket Mortgages).
- All products that change frequently due to flexible infrastructure of cloud computing.

Bass's model was useful in the early 1960s, 1970s and 1980s because most of the major innovations were independent of one another. Early television sets and telephones were essentially durable goods, and they had very few substitutes. Now we can watch "TV" on a laptop, phone, virtual/augmented reality headset and/or at a local bar. Televisions themselves are also changing significantly every few years as their resolution, connectivity and intelligence increases.

Forecasting technology adoption cannot be done with twentieth century differential equations, though this is not to say we cannot predict adoption rates: entropy may be increasing, but so are our modeling abilities.

Modeling today is now done with data scientists and analytics. No single model can be applied to describe disruptive technologies, in general, and if such a model existed, it would be proprietary and immediately sold to hedge funds and government intelligence analysts. Instead, researchers try their best to predict single events based on the data they have.

Quantitative modeling of technology adoption rates can no longer be done on a wide-scale basis, but rather only through focused lenses with the help of skilled expertise and modern analytical tools.

What about the *qualitative/conceptual models* of technology adoption? Are they still useful? For those less mathematically inclined, can we still explain rapid technology adoption—if not model it—through historical theories?

Diffusion of Innovations

Most business professionals are not quantitative Jedi Knights with predictive skill sets. They often operate around basic knowledge and outsource the rest. This modus operandi is why a lot of management reduces to *feel*, making decisions based on intuition and a current knowledge base, amid certain ambiguity.

A Google search of *technology adoption* quickly reveals that most people think about technology adoption through the lens of the diffusion theory of technology adoption created in the 1960s by Everett Rogers (1962). The theory postulates six categories of users (approximately) normally distributed across the categories (Figure 2.1).

The curve is predicated on technology capability and the adopter's tolerance for risk. As already discussed, the conventional *assumption* is that technology evolves at a pace that justifies phased adoption. Early deployments are assumed to be relatively risky—but potentially high pay off—because the technology is likely not fully baked.

Later adoption is safer, especially if a company is part of the *early* or *late* majority (the 68%) and has prior experience that justifies their approach to technology adoption, that is, they've not *suffered* because they were *late* or *punished* because they were early.

Rogers' theory makes practical sense when looking at selected quantitative examples such as the adoption of *iPods* from 2002 to 2014 (Figure 2.2).

When the *iPod* was first introduced, consumers were either still listening to their portable CD players or were early adopters of MP3 devices. After Steve Job's proclamation about *1,000 songs in your pocket*, Apple was propelled into a decade of dominance in the music industry. Many did not forecast Apple's success, though consumer behavior followed a predictable pattern that dates all the way back to the 1960s.

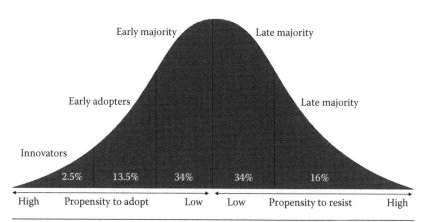

Figure 2.1   The DOI technology adoption curve. (From Rogers, E.M., *Diffusion of Innovations*, Free Press, New York, 1962.)

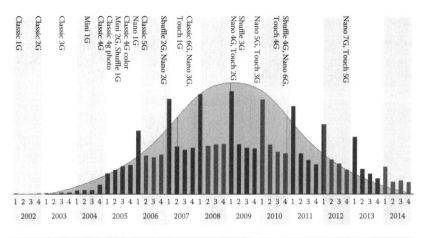

Figure 2.2 Quarterly *iPod* sales, 2002–2014.

Here is a trip down memory lane for Apple fans:

- From 2001–2005, Apple released the iPod classic and iPod mini (early adopters bought)
- From 2006–2009, Apple released the Shuffle, Nano and Touch (and now everyone wanted to have an iPod)
- After 2009, the iPhone began to gain popularity, cannibalizing some of the sales and leaving the remainder to be driven by users who had neither smartphones nor portable music players (think parents and grandparents)

This adoption pattern suggests that Rogers' diffusion of innovation *worked* because

- It sounds reasonable.
- It's easy to think of other examples of products or technologies that have come to market and followed this pattern.
- It's convenient (there is plenty of literature to back it up).

But the problem with the diffusion of innovation framework may be the basis of one's technology adoption toolset that's quickly becoming obsolete.

Here is why we should quickly adjust our thinking: the adoption of *iPods* was a business-to-consumer (B2C) event—not business-to-business (B2B)—a world where different rules apply. The B2B adoption curve assumes up-front requirements due diligence where business requirements are well understood and well defined before candidate technologies are vetted.

This is the essence of the old technology adoption curve—*requirements-first/technology-second*. We know that if the need for elaborate and validated requirements was reduced, adoption rates would increase.

When we analyzed Apple's sales of smartphones and tablets just a few years later, we saw significantly higher—*and faster*—adoption rates (Figure 2.3).

Within 11 weeks, Apple sold 8 million more *iPhones* than *iPods*, and more than 22 million *iPads* per quarter! *From a cumulative standpoint, within the first 11 quarters of its product launch, Apple sold 3 million iPods, 42 million iPhones and 121 million iPads.*

When technologies are adopted at such a rate, the ability to categorize and define customers through adopter categories in the diffusion of innovations framework is difficult and impractical.

It also means that adopter categories are less definable than they previously were. The categories blur as organizations increase their appetite for risk as depicted in Figure 2.4.

The difficulty of blurring or disappearing adopter categories is marketing. Adopter categories were previously a way of loosely defining customer segments. By clustering customers based on similar adoption characteristics, marketers could strategically adjust their marketing and sales strategies.

The implications of a shift toward more early adoption are many. Similar to a chain reaction, this shift catalyzes itself: a sustained population of early adopters converts to an increased market potential for innovation, which ultimately fuels innovation itself (Figure 2.5).

The more early buyers there are, the more successful start-ups can be, and the more successful startups there are and the more successful startups there are, the more potential entrepreneurs and investors adjust their risk/reward ratios, increasing the number of startups—which increases innovation and disruption: early adoption is a self-fulfilling best practice.

If you are at a large company in an industry susceptible to disruption, this can be concerning. When modeling is difficult, and fundamental theories of adoption are impractical, if not outright wrong, many business professionals turn to subject matter experts (SMEs).

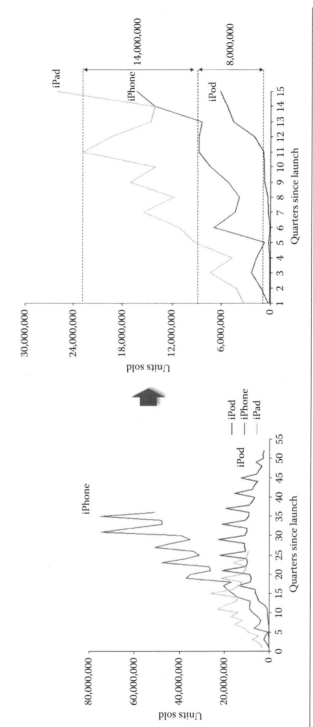

Figure 2.3   Apple sales in the early 2000s. (Apple quarterly reports.)

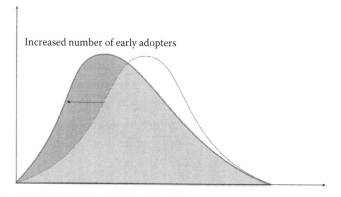

Figure 2.4   New adoption curve.

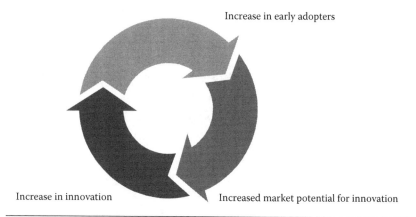

Figure 2.5   Implication of sustained early adoption rates.

But how good are contracted consultants at explaining and predicting the future? Are their proprietary models any better than those from academia?

The Gartner Hype Cycle

Companies often seek subject matter expertise from third party research and advisory firms as part of their due diligence around ET trends. Gartner specifically has been widely cited and publicized in the past decade by creating captivating visuals such as the *magic quadrant* and the *hype cycle*. The famous *hype cycle* is a graphical representation of the maturity and adoption of emerging technologies.

Jackie Fenn and Raskino (2008) describe the creation of the model like this:

> The hype cycle was started as a single Gartner research note I published in 1995, making the observation that technologies tend to follow this cycle of over-enthusiasm and disillusionment, prior to a deeper understanding of where they really apply. I added some examples of technologies on to the chart to illustrate the point. The following year, I started getting requests from clients to *update* the hype cycle with the current year's emerging technologies, which I did, and it became an annual event.

A further description of Gartner's over-enthusiasm-and-disillusionment approach is outlined in the following steps:

1. *Technology trigger*: It occurs after a public announcement or demonstration of the product is made public. Awareness about the technology then starts to spread and attracts first media coverage. Venture capitalists and early adopting companies then aim to capitalize on possible first mover advantages.
2. *Peak of inflated expectations*: This phase is characterized by high expectations boosted or hyped further by media coverage. Following a bandwagon effect, companies invest without having a clear strategy or sound business case.
3. *Trough of disillusionment*: The overenthusiasm and hyped investments result in commercial adoptions that fail to meet performance and/or revenue expectations. Public disappointments spread and are again hyped by media, this time negatively.
4. *Slope of enlightenment*: Some early adopters who continued working with the technology begin to experience net benefits and regain motivation. With more investments, the contextual understanding of the technology grows, resulting in increasing performance. The technology begins to be socialized.
5. *Plateau of productivity*: The technology is realistically valued. Following successful market place demonstrations, the adoption accelerates.

The mostly common use cases for this categorization are:

- Helping to optimize emerging technology investment decisions.
- Helping to uncover drivers that will make a new technology commercially rewarding.
- Aiding in the balancing of business benefits and associated risks.

One reason why the model has become so popular is its simplicity. Clients can see in a single chart how different emerging technologies are as compared to one another.

Unfortunately, the trade-off for simplicity is clarity and accuracy.

Several studies have indicated that there is little mathematical evidence or explanation of where specific technologies are even placed on the curve—which leads to frequent miscategorizations (Murugesan, 2009; Steinert and Leifer, 2010).

For example, in 2005, the technology at the very top of the hype cycle was *business process management* (*BPM*) suites. Now, over a decade later, *BPM* has completely overcome the hype. Similarly, in 2002, *personal digital assistant phones* were on the decline, which is of course amusing to those of you reading this on your smartphone.

We have included a more thorough analysis of changes in different emerging technologies along with Gartner's hype cycle (Figure 2.6).

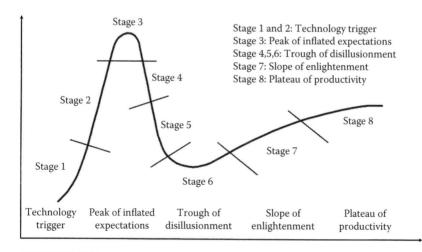

Figure 2.6 Hype cycle segmentation methodology.

The hype cycle is riddled with instances where technologies do not follow a linear progression between stages, but rather jump back and forth. There are also instances of technologies that go through several cycles of disappearance and reappearance at later dates (e.g., Biometric Sensors).

The Obsolescence of Traditional Technology Adoption Models

Historical adoption models are not very useful today. Companies have a set of adoption processes they either choose to follow or abandon as the environment around them changes.

We know that many companies react to their competitors' adoption patterns: if everyone in an industry is adopting a certain technology, odds are that everyone will look to their market leaders to establish a set of *best practices*.

These *best practices* are usually based on previous views of technology adoption discussed earlier in this chapter: early deployments are assumed to be risky—but potentially high pay off—because brand new technologies are not fully baked. Consumers and organizations thus respond to these new technological entrants by either adopting immediately because they have a high tolerance/appetite for risk (the minority) or they wait so that to avoid the consequences of unwise early investment decisions.

The three major stages in the adoption process consist of an initial adoption stage in which IT requirements and capabilities are analyzed, as well as the readiness of the organization. Next, based on this initial prework, a go/no-go decision is made and the implementation stage begins. Here the actual deployment occurs supported by the various stakeholders in the organization. After a successful technology adoption, the technology moves into operational and postadoption stages in which continuous improvement and upgrades occur.

This process requires several steps, where each step defines the next (which is why the adoption process is often historically described as *phased*). IT organizations were and often still are deliberately organized around these sets of overarching technology acquisitions, deployment and support processes. Some focus on a *plan/build/run* strategy, whereas others focus on some sort of elaborate requirements modeling and demand management.

These strategies made sense in the twentieth century because technology costs were high, implementation times were lengthy, and technology often entered the market at an immature state.

Obsolescence needs context. It also needs to be described. Here are two arguments for the replacement of traditional technology adoption models.

Replacement Argument 1—A Decrease in Change Agent Headaches

The successful adoption of new technology is directly tied to the stakeholders that manage the decision process. Everett Rogers (1962) stated that a change agent with established credibility is required to convince fellow stakeholders that the new technology has a relative advantage over an existing technology or its alternatives. The new technology must be compatible and demonstrable. The technology also generally needs to demonstrate a strong use case to get the backing of financially minded stakeholders.

What made this difficult historically was the fact that IT expenses were previously viewed as *operational* and were unable to demonstrate compelling strategic return on investment (ROI). Because of this, the change agent (often the Chief Information Officer, CIO, or Chief Technology Officer, CTO) would inevitably have to fight an uphill battle against an army of budget constraints, hesitant senior managers and disapproving shareholders.

Today, IT expenditures are often *very* strategic. CEOs and corporate steering committees are increasingly aware that their competitive success is directly linked to their ability to utilize data and new technologies.

IT adoption is no longer a topic of contention, but rather a subject for board room consideration. Analytics, mobile devices and cloud computing—*among so many emerging and disruptive technologies*—have fundamentally changed how many organizations go-to-market resulting in a decrease in stakeholder arguments.

In fact, many CEO's are so eager to outpace their competition that they may, in fact, be adopting technologies without even a baseline understanding of their full strategic implications.

Replacement Argument 2—Requirements Testing Is Over
(and for Good Reason)

Figure 2.7 suggests that before companies decide to adopt new technologies there is a period of intense internal due diligence in which companies map their technological requirements as if their very existence depended on it.

Requirements analyses are still long and tiring processes. Depending on the size of the company, hundreds, even thousands of system requirements might be developed and tested along with the inputs of numerous stakeholders. At the end of this lengthy process, there are total cost of ownership (TCO) and ROI calculations that inform a go/no-go decision.

Despite how rigorous requirements analyses might be, IT projects have an alarmingly high failure rate. For example, according to McKinsey & Company (2016):

> 17% of large IT projects go so badly that they threaten the very existence of the company. Furthermore, 45% of these projects were over budget, 7% went over time, while delivering 56% less value than predicted on average.

The reasons for such a high failure rate among technology implementation projects are numerous. Some of the more widely cited reasons include poor project management, uncommitted senior management support and poor project *scope creep*. However, the largest reason is nearly always traceable to poor requirements analyses.

Just look at the following statistics collected during a 13-year period beginning in 1995:

- Requirements problems have been proven to contribute to 20%–25% of all project failures: the average project overran its budget 189% and its schedule by 22% (Chaos Report/The Standish Group, 1995).
- Requirements errors account for 70%–85% of rework (Liffingwell, 1997).
- Poor requirements account for 71% of project failures (Grady, 2005).
- Between 40% and 60% of all software defects can be attributed to bad requirements (Carmel and Abbott, 2006).

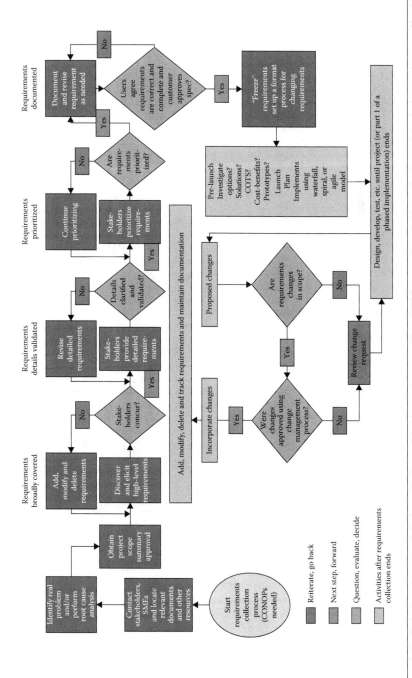

Figure 2.7 Typical requirements elicitation, collection and development process. (From MITRE corporation, eliciting, collecting and developing requirements, March 2016.)

- Only 34% of projects expected to finish on time; 52% had proposed functionality; 82% had time overruns; 43% had budget overruns (The Chaos Chronicles/Standish Group, 2004).
- Flawed requirements trigger 70% of project failures (Greene, 2005).
- Gaps in the technical requirements accounted for more than 70% of program problems (United States Government Accountability Office, 2008).

Large-scale enterprise resource planning (ERP) projects are the poster children of failure. Depending on the size of the company, ERP implementations can cost upward of hundreds of millions of dollars, and can take anywhere between 2 and 5 years to implement.

Today, however, instead of worrying about in-house data storage capabilities, data security, or even infrastructure needs, many companies have now opted for cloud-based services that are often outsourced to third-party specialists. This has virtually transformed the adoption timeline from years to months—and avoided some of the biggest ERP disasters in history.

Historic Strategy Formation

Any good technology adoption process should be aligned with a company's competitive strategy. A well-developed corporate strategy will determine how much risk an organization is willing to take, what types of technologies they need to become successful, and how much budget they're willing to allocate. Changes in technology adoption will ultimately stem from a combination of innovative thinking from a company's ground troops as well as from their generals looking to capture additional market share.

As suggested throughout this book, two of the most influential and well-known strategy books written about strategic technology adoption in the twentieth century were the *The Innovator's Dilemma* by Clayton Christensen (1997) and *Crossing the Chasm* by Geoffrey Moore (1991). Although few comparisons between the two works have been done, they are virtually two sides of the same coin. Geoffrey Moore argued that companies will succeed by choosing a niche market that they can dominate and can use to attack adjacent markets.

Christensen said that companies are prone to disruption from companies that attack from the foothold of the market, where they have perfected their product with low-margin customers and found a way to accelerate their innovation's performance.

Christensen and Moore's theories were born in the 1990s, and used case studies of the disk drive market and Kodak—not *Uber* or *iPads*. Are their assumptions still applicable in the early 2000s?

Here is an overview of the frameworks.

Crossing the Chasm

As mentioned previously, one of the largest criticisms of Rogers' diffusion of innovations theories (1962) was that it offered little prescriptive recourse for business management. Moore sought to solve this problem in 1991 in his book *Crossing the Chasm*, which assumes that each adopter group has a unique view of adoption and that companies need to adjust their marketing tactics accordingly to meet each segment's needs.

Moore noticed that a disproportionate number of innovation failures occur when company customer bases are transitioning from early adopters to early majority. Early majority adopters tend to be most difficult to capture as they are intense *pragmatists*. This pragmatism presents a dilemma for companies: early majority customers don't want to buy from a company until it has become fully established; however, that company can't become established until they have generated meaningful sales. The successful capture of early majority customer segments is the best indicator of whether an innovation can dominate the market. Moore referred to this gap between early adopters and early majority customers as *the chasm* and devised a strategy to leap over the chasm.

His strategy suggested that start-ups find tiny underserved markets that they can leverage to *bowl* through a set of niche markets, *hide* while they perfect their technology and then build relationships with pragmatic, value-based customers. Moore hypothesized that when a certain amount of underserved niche markets are captured, the market would shift to a new (disruptive) architecture, putting the start-up at the center of a technology tornado.

The key to Moore's assumption is the initial product positioning and market segmentation. The first targeted niche market needs to naturally progress to other markets and positioning them depends on where the product is within the technology life cycle. For example, marketing teams should focus on a minimal initial stance such as *name it and frame it* for visionary/technology enthusiasts versus a *compete and differentiate* approach for more conservative and pragmatic customer segments.

Once revenue streams have reached double or even triple digit growth, most business leaders only focus on trying to maintain growth. Companies don't fully conquer one niche market at a time; instead, they attack a small portion in each of the 5 or 10 segments they identified. This approach is fatal because winning a small portion of each group will create no word of mouth effect, and prevent the vendor from strategically adjusting their marketing positioning to address competitive threats. After a few years of intense growth from chasing sales, vendors will inevitably fall victim to their own excitement and see their revenues plummet down a chasm of their own doing.

Are companies as blinded or greedy as Moore suggests?

Perhaps companies aren't following Moore's principles for a simpler reason: they can't. Our hypothesis is that adoption categories are blurring and perhaps fading all together. If this hypothesis holds true then segmenting customer groups or even just distinguishing between early adopters and early majority customers would be virtually impossible.

The Innovator's Dilemma – Plus Solution

Christensen also agrees that chasing after sales can be detrimental to a company's innovation success. In fact, he says that the fundamental concepts of traditional business management are contradictory to being innovative. *The Economist* praised *The Innovator's Dilemma* as being one of the six most influential business books of all time. But Christensen's theory is much narrower than what many believe, despite being widely applied.

The Innovator's Dilemma identifies two types of innovation:

1. *Sustaining innovation (majority of innovations)*: When companies improve what they already have, making their product more appealing and useful to their existing customers.

2. *Disruptive innovation*: Innovations that begin at the foothold of the market, meaning that they service the low-margin, fringe customers, who have lower expectations on product performance. By definition, disruptive innovation is not as good as the existing technology.

The theory is based on the assumption that companies of different sizes will define their capabilities and markets differently. Following sound management principles, industry leaders will focus on their best customers and products with the highest margins. Large companies need larger markets to keep growing, so they invest their time and resources accordingly.

However, as Christensen notes:

> Firms that succeed in one generation of innovation almost inevitably become hamstrung by their own success and are thus doomed to lose out in the next wave of innovation.

This is because improving a current product takes time, money and iteration. Once a product has reached the mass market, improvements are incremental and have only diminishing returns as seen in proverbial S-curve.

Market leaders in this situation often have the luxury of having huge customer sets to rely on which mitigates the loss of inpatient customers wanting for faster innovators. However, they're also burdened by the expectations of high yearly sales due to their large customer bases. This causes market leading companies to pass on investing in small niche markets that don't yield immediate ROIs.

Although rejecting investment in these new technologies is often in the market leader's best fiduciary interest due to their margin pressures and cost structures, it gives room to smaller companies to occupy the lower margin markets with poorer products. Their nimbleness and low-cost structures allows them to operate sustainably where the market leader could not, and experiment with their offerings.

Initially these small start-ups don't pose a threat—however, once they improve their product positioning and value proposition, they may reach a stage where their offering is good enough for everyone. In many cases, the entry-point markets are left behind as the new technologies move into higher margin upmarket territory, disrupting the previous market leader.

Christensen's most cited case study example is disk drives. The 3.5 inch disk drives are entered at the foot of 5.25 inch disk drive market, because they didn't have the capacity or speed needed for mainstream customers (who only wanted better mainframe computers). Producers of 5.25 inch disk drives continue to improve their product, whereas new companies that were producing 3.5 inch disk drives were focused to find new customers and markets. These new entrants then started selling their disks to early laptop producers such as Compaq, a market that previous disk drive producers considered to be too risky. The 3.5 disk drive producers were then able to rapidly improve the performance of their product, overtake the 5.25 inch disk drive market and eventually drive the 5.25 producers out of the market.

Christensen's theory is less focused on whether a technology is disruptive at a given point in time, but rather whether it is following a disruptive trajectory. Netflix started at the low-end of the market, serving only fringe customers willing to wait several days for a DVD to arrive, and not necessarily concerned with new releases. Netflix did not go for the mainstream market initially. Over time, they increased their selection of DVD's far beyond what blockbuster made available, and then moved into online streaming, eventually attacking the mainstream.

So how can large, market-leading companies protect themselves from these small nimble start-ups that come from the foothold of the market? Should they invest in innovation labs or skunk work projects?

It's a difficult question to answer because when disruptive innovations start at the low-end of the market, their market size and returns are small. This presents a problem for any company trying to fund a disruptive product or business unit as their financial health will inevitably be riskier due to the uncertainty of the venture.

Money invested into new growth initiatives is usually money well spent, so long as the core of the business is healthy. However, if the core business is under pressure to perform, this new investment may turn into a potentially financial toxic strain. What further complicates and worsens the situation is when a company finds itself in financial duress. Then the growth venture is deemed necessary for survival and is forced to grow very big, very fast. This pressure fundamentally contradicts the iterative process needed for the growth venture to properly take hold of the market.

Christensen argues that new growth businesses should be launched regularly, but only when the core business is healthy. In fact, the best time to invest in growth is when the company is growing.

Next, as an organization grows, Christensen says that companies should continue to divide up their business units, so that each unit can launch new ventures and be small enough to benefit from small opportunities. Managers should also be keen to minimize the use of profit from the core business to subsidize potential losses. Once a venture is profitable, it remains likely to continue to do so even when the core business is struggling.

Finally, Christensen makes several points around human capital. Company employees, starting from senior executives all the way to marketing, sales and engineering teams should be coached in disruptive innovation, so that they can spot opportunities or be confident enough to invest or divest from a potential venture.

Which companies are doing this now—if any? Should companies double down on Christensen's strategies given the recent shifts in adoption rates? Or should they approach adoption differently?

3

RAPID TECHNOLOGY ADOPTION IN THE TWENTY-FIRST CENTURY

Technology adoption has always been challenging to technologists, business managers and executives. They grapple with the selection and timing to pilot specific technologies, and the methods, tools and techniques necessary to successfully pilot and then deploy new technologies.

We know that in the twentieth century, technology adoption was slow and deliberate, almost always preceded by an elaborate requirements analysis validated by business *users* who needed some functionality enabled by software or communications technology (Brooks, 1987; Boehm, 1988; Davis, 1990; Dorfman and Thayer, 1997; Faulk, 1997; Wiegers, 2003). But the pace of technology change, a sharp increase in *Shadow IT*, competitive pressures and quick cloud delivery combined to challenge the old technology adoption process.

We conducted a survey and series of interviews in 2016 and 2017 to understand technology adoption today. We concentrated on emerging (and potentially disruptive) technology and surveyed and interviewed over 150 directors, managers and executives across multiple vertical industries about how they were tracking, piloting and adopting emerging technologies.

The survey was hosted in various places, but principally at the Cutter Consortium, a technology research and consulting organization based in Arlington, Massachusetts (www.cutter.com) as well as via *Forbes Magazine*, www.andriole.com and several social media sites. The survey polled business *and* technology professionals. Interviews were conducted with a subset of additional participants (beyond those surveyed). The interviews were conducted with a consistent set of questions.

The most significant finding is the death of detailed requirements analysis and modeling: more and more companies are trying-before-they-buy, often placing technology-first and requirements-second—a huge departure from technology adoption in the twentieth century. Another significant finding is the rank ordering of the specific emerging technologies that companies believe have the greatest potential and the technologies they plan to pilot.

Again, the survey and interview data revealed—among other findings—the following:

- Companies have thrown the old (slow, deliberate) technology adoption models and processes out the window: defined requirements have given way to experimental pilots, and many companies have placed technology potential ahead of requirements-driven applications.
- The whole notion of *technology adoption categories*—such as *innovators, early adopters, early majority, late majority* and *laggards*—is obsolete: those who worried about *crossing the chasm* (Moore, 1991) appear to have no knowledge of what the concept even means.
- Shadow IT *won* the spending war because it's no longer possible for enterprise IT to control technology adoption: cloud delivery has made it possible for business units to rapidly pilot and deploy emerging and disruptive technology independently with no coordination with corporate or enterprise IT.
- Companies know which technologies they want to pilot: they believe that there's platinum in analytics and cloud computing, gold in BYOD, wearables, e-Payment systems and e-Learning technologies but, perhaps surprisingly, only silver in automated reasoning.
- Companies now have as many federated, decentralized and *other* governance structures as centralized ones—a major change from the twentieth century.
- Companies are rushing their pilots even if it means failing to measure success or failure: less than 30% have ROI measurement processes in place around their emerging technology pilots.

- Due to the pace of technology change, competitive fear, cost pressures and ongoing commitments to digital transformation, emerging technology adoption—without detailed requirements analyses—will accelerate.
- Technology and digital transformation consultants will exploit trends toward *technology-first-versus-requirements-second* pilots accelerating technology adoption.
- Rapid technology adoption will become a way of life for twenty-first century companies and the *professionalization* of technology adoption will continue to increase dramatically.

Here are the five major hypotheses and five questions that defined the research:

Hypotheses:

1. Due to the unprecedented pace of technology change, conventional, staged and requirements-driven technology adoption models are changing—and probably disappearing altogether.
2. Emerging and potentially disruptive technology is adopted very differently, much faster and less purposefully than technologies that were previously vetted and deployed.
3. *Consumerization*, cloud computing and shared governance have emerged as the major drivers of emerging business technology adoption, and that personal technology quickly becomes professional technology, often delivered overnight by cloud providers directly accessible to business units.
4. The decoupling of technology solutions away from integrated technology platforms (such as ERP and DBMS platforms) is rapidly progressing, especially due to the emergence and availability of infrastructure (IaaS) and applications (SaaS) cloud delivery.
5. New technology adoption models will be *instant* and *continuous*, and distinctions among adoption categories (Rogers, 1962: innovators/early adopters/early majority/late majority/laggards) will blur and eventually vanish, replaced by whole new technology adoption approaches, models and best practices.

Interview questions:

1. *Are you still anchored in* requirements-first/technology-second *technology adoption processes?*
2. *What would happen if you threw the SDLC out the window— and just brought all kinds of new technologies into the company and started to pilot them?*
3. *In your view, are technologies/platforms/devices such as iPads, social media and analytics* ready to go?
4. *How much Shadow IT is there at your company? Does Shadow IT fuel emerging technology adoption? Should you shut it down? Or should you let it go?*
5. *What new/emerging/ready/disruptive technologies are high on your list? Which ones do you think have been overhyped?*

Findings

A traditional industry survey instrument was used to collect data and conduct face-to-face and e-mail administered interviews (see Appendices A and B for the survey questions, interviewee questions and selected interviewee responses).

More than 150 different respondents (133) and interviewees (19) answered a variety of questions about technology adoption. Their functions were split among different types of industries and business and technology professionals in positions ranging from analysts to the C-suite. The majority of the respondents came from companies with small- to medium-sized technology teams; health care and financial services were our most represented industries, though others were well represented.

The 150 respondents and interviewees were *not* mostly from the digital world. In fact, they were widely dispersed across the technology, business and finance communities: slightly *more* business professionals participated than technology professionals. In both the business and technology sectors, most of the respondents were analysts/directors/senior directors (26%) and managers (29%).

Specializations of the respondents varied with the majority coming from digital technology (34%), finance and accounting (18%), innovation (15%) and *other technology* (15%).

We assumed the respondents would be from companies with large technology staffs, but the largest percentage of respondents (37%) were from companies with small technology teams (1–50 professionals), primarily in the finance and health care industries. Although at the time we did not see this distribution as significant, the results clearly suggest that companies with smaller technology teams are more flexible than those with larger teams. This speaks to how size, governance and entrenchment influence attitudes about change (Figure 3.1).

One of the hypotheses we tested was that conventional, staged and requirements-driven technology adoption models are changing—and probably disappearing altogether. We asked four questions about adoption processes and requirements analysis (Figure 3.2).

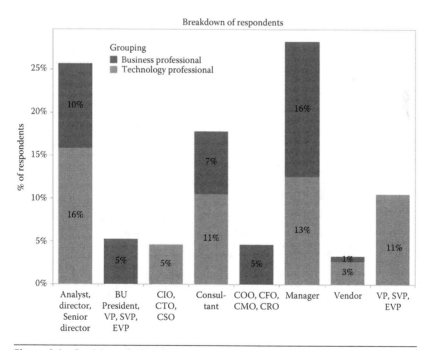

Figure 3.1 Breakdown of respondents.

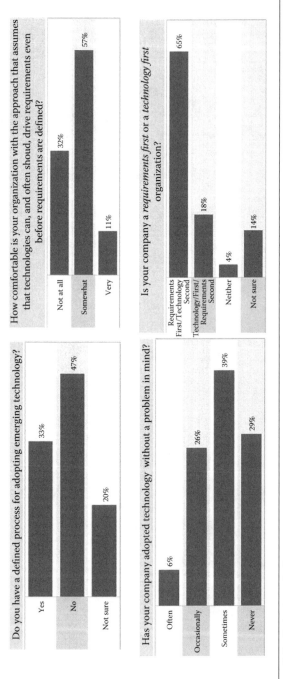

Figure 3.2   Technology adoption processes.

The answers were surprising:

- Only 33% of the companies in our survey have a defined process for the adoption of emerging technology and 68% were very or somewhat comfortable with a *technology first/ requirements second* approach to emerging technology adoption.
- Amazingly, 71% of the respondents believe that technology can often/occasionally/sometimes be deployed without a specific problem in mind.
- Even more surprising, 62% of the organizations that indicated there are not comfortable that technologies can drive requirements have adopted emerging/disruptive technology without a specific problem in mind.

We asked about how companies were rethinking and redefining their approach to requirements before-versus-after emerging technology adoption. The notion that companies are willing to throw old approaches to requirements analysis and modeling out in favor of technology-driven adoption would have been summarily rejected in the twentieth century. Figure 3.3 presents the results.

The results speak directly to the onslaught of emerging technologies and the need to remain agile and competitive. The responses suggest that technology (not requirements) is *winning* the adoption race and many companies are willing to explore, prototype and pilot emerging technologies even if they've failed to identify the problems the technologies might solve.

The findings challenge the traditional technology adoption process: *the very idea that technologies would be acquired and deployed—however*

		Adopted ET without specific problems in mind?			
		Never	Sometimes	Occasionally	Often
Is your organization comfortable that technologies can drive requirements before requirements are defined?	Not at all		38%	33%	26%	3%
	Somewhat		26%	44%	26%	4%
	Very		13%	33%	27%	27%

Figure 3.3 Requirements-driven versus rapid adoption.

carefully—without documented and validated requirements, flies in the face of what technology and business professionals defined as "best practice" for decades.

The survey and interview data suggest that companies are reacting to the pace of technology change, consumerization and the immediate need for digital transformation with new approaches to technology adoption. But, as suggested in Figure 3.2, 65% of companies still consider their business to be a *requirements first/technology second* type of organization. This may be an indication of corporate lag time: although organizations are comfortable with experimenting with new technologies, as Figure 3.3 suggests, they're hesitant to fully reject the traditional models and processes they've practiced for decades.

But the data in Figure 3.4 clearly describe the shift from requirements-first to technology-first: respondents were perfectly split on the primacy of requirements versus technology.

What are the drivers of emerging technology adoption? Figures 3.5 and 3.6 report the findings regarding technology adoption drivers and the impact *Shadow IT* (unauthorized corporate spending on technology) has on technology adoption.

We hypothesized that the major drivers of emerging technology adoption were cloud computing, shared governance and *consumerization*. The data described the influence of *Shadow IT* and consumerization (51% of the respondents reported that Shadow IT influenced technology adoption *a lot* or *sometimes*, and 38% of our respondents reported that *consumer product awareness* was a driver of emerging technology adoption). As suspected, Figure 3.6 suggests that there's a range of forces driving the changes in emerging technology adoption in different industries. Industries such as consumer, media and retail are more open to the idea of adopting emerging

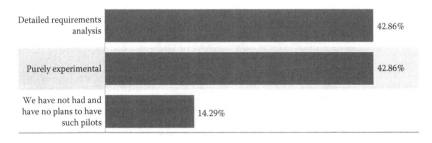

Figure 3.4   Defined requirements versus technology experiments.

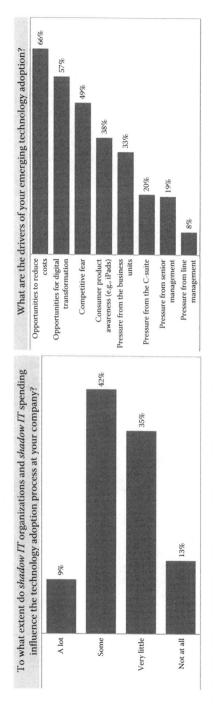

Figure 3.5   Emerging technology adoption drivers.

What are the drivers of your emerging technology adoption?

	Opportunities to reduce costs	Opportunities for digital transformation	Competitive fear	Consumer product awareness (e.g., iPads)	Pressure from the business units	Pressure from the C-suite	Pressure from senior management	Pressure from line management
Automotive	50%	100%	50%	0%	0%	0%	0%	0%
Banking	50%	33%	67%	0%	17%	17%	0%	0%
Consulting	43%	29%	29%	57%	43%	29%	43%	0%
Consumer	100%	100%	100%	50%	0%	0%	0%	0%
Education	44%	67%	22%	33%	33%	22%	11%	11%
Energy	80%	80%	20%	40%	20%	0%	0%	0%
Engineering	80%	20%	80%	0%	0%	0%	0%	0%
Financial services	63%	69%	50%	38%	38%	25%	19%	6%
Food and beverage	100%	33%	0%	67%	67%	33%	0%	67%
Government	83%	100%	33%	67%	0%	0%	0%	0%
Health Care	77%	46%	54%	38%	46%	31%	31%	8%
Insurance	33%	67%	67%	33%	33%	33%	0%	0%
Manufacturing	40%	40%	40%	60%	60%	0%	20%	20%
Media	100%	100%	50%	50%	50%	50%	50%	50%
Pharmaceuticals	80%	40%	60%	40%	60%	20%	40%	0%
Retail	100%	50%	0%	0%	0%	50%	0%	0%
Technology services	71%	79%	71%	57%	36%	21%	21%	7%
Telecommunications	50%	25%	50%	25%	25%	13%	13%	13%
Transportation	100%	50%	0%	50%	50%	0%	0%	0%

Figure 3.6 Emerging technology adoption drivers of across industries.

technology to reduce costs and to enable digital transformation. In fact, Figure 3.5 indicates that 66% of all respondents considered emerging technology because it might lower technology costs and 57% because it might enable digital transformation. 49% feared the competition and looked to emerging technology as a path to enhance their value propositions.

Our hypothesis about shared governance was also confirmed. Figure 3.6 shows respondents on average reported *pressure from the business units* 13% more frequently than *pressure from senior management* or *pressure from the C-suite*. This is especially noteworthy because only 20% of our respondents lived in federated governance structures (versus 57% who lived in centralized structures).

Figure 3.7 provides further credence to our hypothesis; one-third of the companies in our survey with centralized governance models have adopted emerging technology because it faced pressure from their business units. This finding challenges the traditional power structures of IT governance and suggests that business units are affecting even the most consolidated governance models. In fact, if you look across the different governance structures, we can clearly see that companies are exhibiting more *shared governance* behavior by adopting emerging technology due to pressures other than from the C-suite. Across the board, with the obvious exception of a decentralized structure, we can see that pressure from business units outpaces pressure either from the C-suite or from the senior management as drivers for emerging technology adoption.

Figure 3.8 is further proof that lines between traditional governance structures are under pressure from the effects of *Shadow IT*. 49% of respondents with centralized structures said that *Shadow IT* has had *a lot* or *some* influence over their companies' technology adoption processes. This effect is not an anomaly as we see it reflected across other structures. This is another indicator that not only are lines blurring among governance structures, but that *shared governance* is more enabling of adopting emerging technology.

We discovered that the vast majority of companies learn about emerging technology from research organizations as well as their own in-house business experts. It's interesting to note that *from your personal network* scores high as well. We see this as another indicator of the effects of consumerization (Figure 3.9).

	Opportunities to reduce costs	Opportunities for digital transformation	Competitive fear	Consumer product awareness (e.g., iPads)	Pressure from the business units	Pressure from the C-suite	Pressure from senior management	Pressure from line management
Centralized	59%	55%	52%	41%	33%	18%	12%	8%
Decentralized	43%	29%	29%	29%	14%	0%	14%	0%
Federated	91%	82%	50%	45%	41%	27%	32%	14%
Hybrid	72%	56%	44%	43%	33%	17%	17%	6%

Figure 3.7 Drivers across IT governance structures.

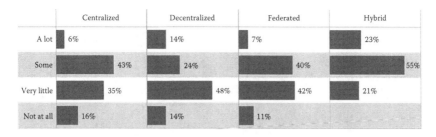

Figure 3.8 Shadow IT influence across governance structures.

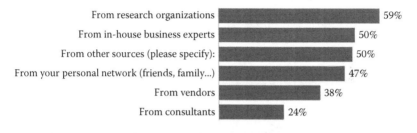

Figure 3.9 Sources of awareness of emerging technology trends.

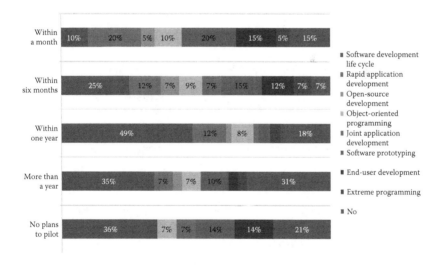

Figure 3.10 Adoption rate and requirements analysis.

We also asked questions about how quickly companies plan to adopt, or have already adopted, emerging/disruptive companies. We analyzed how different characteristics of a company might influence the rate of emerging technology adoption (Figure 3.10).

Figure 3.11 suggests that companies that have methodologies that emphasize flexibility such as rapid application development or

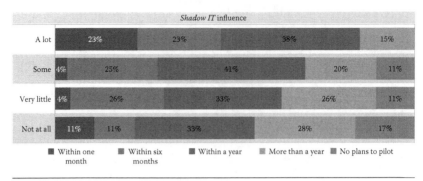

Figure 3.11   Adoption rates and shadow IT influence.

software prototyping adopt emerging technologies the fastest (within a month). This was expected because these methodologies already emphasize relatively rapid adoption over prolonged requirements analysis.

However, when we look at the next fastest adoption rate, the data tell us a whole different story. The software development life cycle (SDLC) methodology, by far, dominates the category for companies that plan to pilot emerging technologies within 6 months after learning about them.

It is remarkable that a company with the SDLC methodology, with its rigid and detailed requirements analysis, comprises the majority of the methodology (and 10% more than the next closest, software prototyping).

This finding is another indicator of how emerging technologies are being adopted rapidly and outside of official adoption frameworks such as SDLC.

Figure 3.11 suggests how strong the influence of *Shadow IT* can be on the adoption rate of emerging technologies. We clearly see the impact of *Shadow IT* on adoption rates. 46% of the companies that are affected by *Shadow IT* a lot plan to pilot emerging technologies within *one month* or *six months* of learning about the technology. This is astounding, given the fact that companies used to take a much longer time to pilot technologies in a requirements-driven adoption model.

Our data also suggest that the budget and manpower of the internal IT department are factors in how fast emerging technologies are piloted. The bigger the internal IT department, the faster the adoption rate often seems to be. Although this may appear in conflict with the conventional wisdom of how larger corporations would be slower to pilot disruptive technologies, we believe that a possible explanation to be that the driving forces we previously mentioned are pushing larger companies (with larger budgets and manpower) to aggressively experiment with emerging technologies.

Adoption rates for emerging technologies seem to be remarkably faster across the governance spectrum (Figures 3.12 and 3.13). 66% of companies with the most rigid of governance structures (Centralized) piloted emerging technologies within *one* or *six* months, or *a year*. This adds to the already abundance of evidence that emerging technologies are adopted in a different, faster model than before regardless of governance structures. Given these *attitudes* about technology adoption

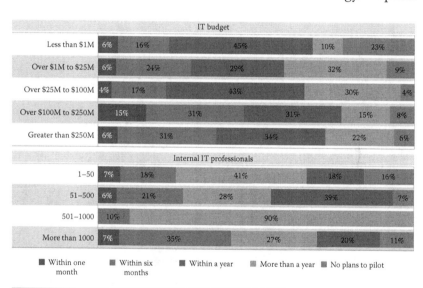

Figure 3.12 Adoption rates and IT budget and professionals.

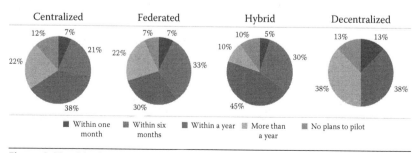

Figure 3.13 Adoption rates and IT governance.

from both technology and business professionals, what emerging technologies are on their pilot lists?

The following are the results of the popularity contest:

1. Cloud computing
2. Structured and unstructured big data analytics
3. e-Learning
4. BYOD (bring-your-own-device)
5. Mobile
6. Wearables
7. Location-based technologies
8. Internet-of-Things (IoT)
9. e-Payment systems
10. Digital security technologies (especially multilayer authentication)

These technologies *won* because they were perceived as the most potentially impactful along the continua of competitive fear, digital transformation and cost reduction—the three most popular reasons to pilot emerging technologies.

Of special note is the variety of planned big data analytics pilots. Several years ago there was barely an understanding of structured versus unstructured data analytics, but today interest is strong in all kinds of analytics, reflecting a much deeper understanding of structured, unstructured, descriptive, explanatory, predictive and even prescriptive analytics.

In fact, two unmistakable intentions are clear: the intention to pilot multiple flavors of cloud computing and several flavors of big data analytics. What's surprising about this finding is not the general interest in cloud computing and analytics, *but the depth of interest in both*, reflected in the specifics within the technology rankings.

Some other technology clusters also stand out, including BYOD, wearables, e-Payment systems and e-Learning technologies.

What *is* surprising is the relative lack of interest in emerging digital security technologies (with a few exceptions) and automated reasoning, because digital security is a core competency of digital transformation and automated reasoning is a foundational technology that enables and extends whole classes of other technologies.

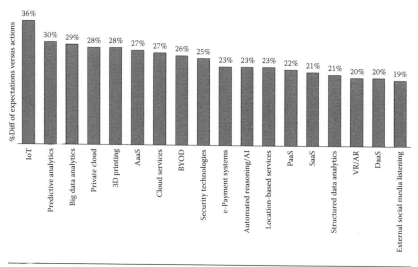

Figure 3.14 Potential versus piloting.

One of the most interesting findings is the relationship between the technologies our respondents *believed* had *great potential* versus the technologies they *intended* to pilot. Figure 3.15 presents the graphic depiction of the distance between potential and piloting.

Looking at the (% Diff) axis in Figure 3.14, it is clear that many companies often see a number of emerging technologies as being potentially useful for their business but often fail to actually pilot them. Some of the top technologies on this list are IoT, predictive analytics, big data analytics and 3D printing. (A matrix of the above data is provided in Figure 3.15.)

Figure 3.15 is one of the survey's reality checks. Recognizing that *talk is cheap*, we designed consistency checks in our survey to test precisely what Figure 3.15 displays.

Figure 3.15 is also a window into the emerging technology watch list that vendors and practitioners should find useful.

We also hypothesized that companies take steps to remain current with the rapid pace of emerging technology. We suggested that companies

1. Aggressively and continuously track technology trends.
2. Optimally organize to exploit the best—and jettison the worst.
3. Continuously and immediately conduct technology pilots.

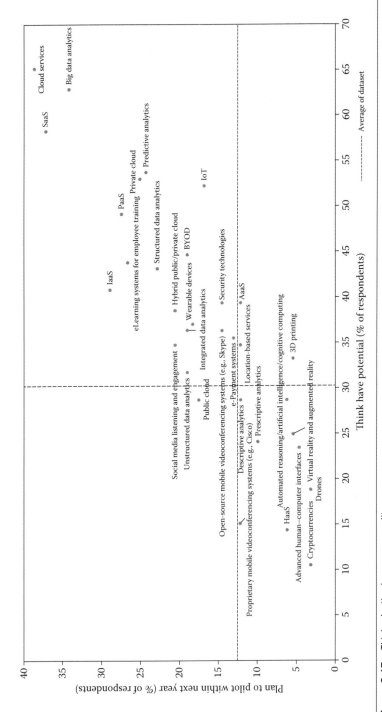

Figure 3.15 Think adoption hype versus reality.

4. Rapidly prioritize, fund and deploy new technologies.

5. Measure TCO and ROI of new technology deployments.

6. Continuously repeat this process.

Is any of this true?

Figure 3.16 presents the data.

The data suggest that companies recognize the need to change their modus operandi around technology adoption, but are sometimes slow to do so. Surprisingly, even though companies understand the potential of emerging technologies, only 27% reported that they were actively maintaining lists of promising emerging/disruptive technologies. (Based on other findings, they appear to be listening passively to suggestions rather than proactively chasing the most promising new technologies.) Roughly 60% reported that they waited a year or longer before piloting some technologies.

Companies then rush to pilot and deploy, *even if it means failing to measure success or failure: only 35% of the companies we surveyed, and less than 25% of the executives we interviewed, quantitatively measured the impact of the emerging technology pilots they undertake.* As the majority of the respondents are from the *business (not technology)* side, the lack of TCO or ROI analyses is especially surprising.

The data suggest that companies are still adjusting to rapid changes and are perhaps slow to digitally transform their adoption processes. *However, the fact that 42% of companies are piloting technologies without detailed requirements analysis, and that the majority no longer follow traditional technology adoption models, indicates there are significant changes underway.*

The data also show a significant increase in the application of formal processes around emerging technologies: 40% of the companies are using innovation labs and creating teams of professionals that specialize in rapid prototyping. *We also found that regulated industries were slower to adopt emerging technology than relatively less regulated ones.* Overall, we expect emerging technology adoption best practices to continue to evolve toward speed, toward technology-first/requirements-second approaches, and toward an emerging technology adoption.

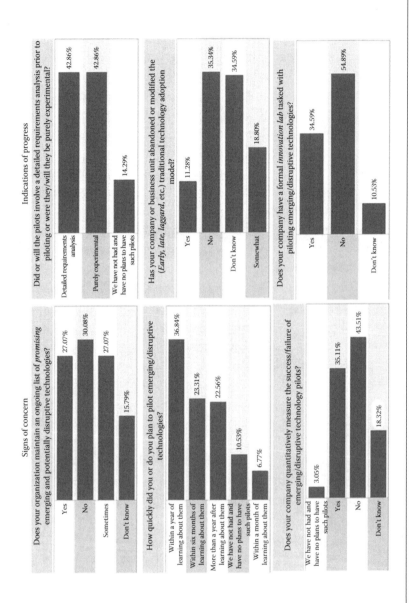

Figure 3.16 Responses to rapid technology change.

Statistical Analysis

The analyses we performed might contain sampling errors due to the limited nature of our data set. Although our goal was to understand the *big picture* of the relationship between the different variables in our survey and the adoption rate of emerging technologies, we nevertheless employed various statistical techniques such as k-fold cross-validation, Fisher's exact test and boosted neural networks to mitigate some of the biases there might be in the data. Appendix C presents the results of these tests.

The New Normal

We concluded from the analysis of the data that emerging technology adoption best practices are very different from old rigid requirements-driven models. Many companies pilot new technologies without rigorous business cases. The new normal for emerging technologies is *technology-first/requirements-second.*

The data suggest that nothing is off-limits: not adoption models, governance structures, or even financial metrics for objectively measuring the impact of emerging technology.

We were surprised to learn that the majority of companies—*nearly 70%*—have already gone to the dark side: *adopting technology without specific, validated requirements.* For many technologies and business professionals, this is still heresy.

Our findings also confirm our core hypotheses about technology adoption: *companies are reacting to the pace of technology change, consumerization and the immediate need for digital transformation with new ways of thinking about how—and how quickly—to adopt emerging technology.*

The rapid pace of emerging technology adoption is occurring in various types of companies. Even companies with an embedded SDLC methodology, or with centralized governance, are not immune to rapid technology adoption.

Lest the *winning* technologies themselves get lost in our analysis of new adoption processes, here's the list (again) of technologies most companies believe has the most potential to transform their businesses:

- Cloud computing
- Structured and unstructured big data analytics
- e-Learning
- BYOD (bring-your-own-device)
- Mobile
- Wearables
- Location-based technologies
- Internet-of-Things (IoT)
- e-Payment systems
- Digital security technologies (especially multilayer authentication)

The dominant theme of our analysis is *change*. The pace of technology and business change has perhaps forever changed the way companies pilot and deploy new technologies. Companies are quickly pursuing emerging technologies—even if it means skipping detailed requirements analysis and avoiding tough questions about ROI.

In fact, technology itself is becoming the hub of all change, because companies literally cannot function without operational, strategic, emerging and even disruptive digital technology. Our research suggests that companies are acknowledging the role that technology plays in operational effectiveness and profitable competitiveness. In fact, every company will eventually become a technology-driven enterprise.

4
THE TECHNOLOGY-
DRIVEN ENTERPRISE

Digital transformation is no longer optional. Companies that want to remain competetive must quickly, creatively and effectively adopt emerging and disruptive technologies. If they fail to leverage these technologies, they will eventually fail. They cannot just place their toes in the water. They must commit to rapid and often immediate technology adoption or they will lose ground to those competitors willing to embrace emerging and disruptive technologies. Fortunately, our data suggest that many companies have already accepted the inevitable.

The organization, delivery, adoption and governance of technology have changed before, but this time the changes are integral to digital transformation. They're also *permanent* if companies wish to remain competitive.

As discussed, our research suggests that there are several drivers of permanent change:

- Accelerating consumerization of technology.
- The number and power of emerging technologies available for immediate adoption.
- Rising competitive fear.
- Continuous digital transformation.
- Participatory, shared federated governance.

There are at least three major organizational outcomes of these drivers:

- Post-federated/decentralized immediate technology adoption.
- Agile technology-enabled business models and processes.
- Continuous digital transformation.

Accelerating Consumerization

Everyone has stories about how personal technology made its way into their companies. The explosion—and availability—of technology capable of solving countless personal productivity and business problems forever changed the technology adoption process. *iPhones* and *iPads* were well in use before technology organizations declared them safe or made them standard issue. The same is true of *Skype and Dropbox* and a growing number of technology-enabled products and services—*especially smartphone apps that have penetrated virtually every business process.* These apps, by the way, are downloaded millions of times a day and directly impact how all of us manage our personal and professional lives.

Consumerization is about a technology repertoire enabled by large and small vendors that sell—*or sometimes gift*—technology directly to individuals. Consumers adopt these technologies on their own and share them among their friends and colleagues. But the difference today is that consumerized technologies can now solve *business* problems quickly and cost-effectively.

Often to the chagrin of the *IT* team, consumerization is now as much a part of technology acquisition and delivery as the *go/no-go* due diligence teams that filled conference rooms for decades. Instead of endless vendor presentations about just how great their technologies are, consumers now routinely try-and-buy technologies quickly and cheaply from the consumerized infrastructure and applications marketplace. App stores are the greatest technology delivery platforms in the world.

These trends are accelerating. More and more of the technology hard at work inside (and outside) companies are embedded in smartphones and tablets. Advertisers, friends, bloggers and family all keep the lists current: look at the number of times new technology is identified by friends versus the number of times it's identified by IT departments.

Employees vote their digital preferences with laptops, tablets, smartphones and applications that make them productive—not from directives from their technology managers. They go to the cloud to store documents and data, host digital meetings and find productive applications. Sometimes these clouds are part of their company's delivery infrastructure—but often they're not. The same employees are also seeking advice in *the crowd* (the consumerized help desk) where opinions, expertise and problem-solving are instantly and continuously available.

Technologies Available for Immediate Adoption

Twentieth century technology adoption models were predicated on the diagnosticity of business requirements and technology maturity. The assumption was that technology and business requirements evolve at a pace that justifies phased adoption. Early deployments were assumed to be risky, costly and therefore unnecessary.

Well-defined business requirements were prized. An enormous industry was created around *requirements analysis, requirements modeling* and *requirements validation*. Books, articles, conferences and workshops were available everywhere. The prevailing wisdom was that business requirements modeling and validation were prerequisites to technology adoption, and that structured pilot demonstrations with compelling TCO and ROI results were necessary to justify deployment. Technologies also had to integrate and interoperate with existing technology infrastructures and architectures. If it failed to cost-effectively integrate, adoption was often halted. If it did integrate, then a transition period was defined to test and deploy the new technology before the technology went into *production*. Finally, *new* technology—just similar to an old technology—required continuous support and expensive refreshes, though today both are often achieved through cloud partners.

As argued throughout this book, technology adoption (and digital transformation) is very different today. *Requirements* are often undefined and adoption is driven by employees–consumers who adopt technologies to solve a variety of known and unknown problems with technologies that are acquired—and sometimes even supported—way outside of the corporate firewall.

Consumer-driven requirements analysis, exploration *and discovery* are the mainstay of rapid and immediate technology adoption. Also note that what we previously described as controlled pilots are today *largely ad hoc opportunistic experiments that sometimes quickly turn into technology deployments—with or without the approval of corporate IT.*

Support is provided by emerging technology vendors who also keep the technology current (even as they perform backups).

There's a growing number of technologies ready to work immediately. Many of these technologies are cloud-based, open source and live outside corporate firewalls. Many of them are easily and inexpensively accessible to corporate professionals and will therefore continue to find their way into companies of all shapes and sizes—regardless of what chief information officers (CIOs) think about the readiness of the technologies.

Competitive Fear

Our research suggests that competitive fear is an important motivator for rapid technology adoption. The pace of technology and business change is so rapid that many companies have no choice but to pilot and deploy technologies that are far from vetted (according to twentieth century due diligence standards). By definition, digital transformation should move fast. There is no question that the number of technology-driven disruptive business models over the past 10 years has fueled this fear especially within traditional industries such as transportation, insurance, health care, entertainment, hospitality and manufacturing.

Digital Transformation

As discussed throughout this book, digital transformation is top of mind for just about every company on the planet. Change is now constant and emerging technology lies at the core of transformation. The five steps to digital transformation discussed in Chapter 2 will help.

But what are the organizational implications?

Participatory, Shared Federated Governance

In the twentieth century, governance was largely about technology standards and control. As we moved into the twenty-first century things began to change, first from centralized to federated and then, more recently, to *participatory*. Governance now involves more stakeholders than it ever did, most of which live outside the corporate firewall. Participatory governance is emerging as the postfederated governance model (Andriole, 2015).

In fully centralized technology organizations, decision rights belong to an enterprise control group; in decentralized organizations, decision rights are diffuse, spread across the enterprise and the business units; and in federated technology organizations, rights are shared across the enterprise, the business units and even specific corporate functions.

Since the mid-1990s, the governance pendulum has swung wildly. In the mid- to late-1990s, technology was considered strategic. After the dot.com bubble burst in 2000, the pendulum swung back to operational control. It stayed that way until 2003 when technology budgets began to increase again. The pendulum swung from operational to strategic again where governance was shared between the enterprise CIO and business unit CIOs (or just the business unit technology directors). We stayed on this course until the world melted down again in 2008—and the governance pendulum swung all the way back to total budget lockdown in which governance was centralized in the hands of a few—or just one—senior executives—such as the CFO, the COO or, infrequently, the CEO.

During all this swinging, something changed. Almost as though it was clandestinely taking advantage of budgetary distractions, technology freed itself from the control of both enterprise and business unit professionals. It escaped the arguments that had it swinging back and forth for decades. In fact, it rendered the word *control* moot: *technology commoditized, consumerized—and left the building.* It also finalized the near-total dependency business has on the reliability, scalability, reach and security of its digital technology. *Put another much simpler way, business cannot function—or even exist—without information technology (IT)—and everyone knew IT.*

Despite warnings and trepidations, business units are now aggressively adopting new technologies. Consumerized, cloud-delivered technology has changed the rules around acquisition, deployment and support. Business units no longer ask corporate IT if they can rent software (or buy *iPads*). They just rent and buy as they choose—often without even telling IT for what they've done.

Shadow IT is bigger than ever. The ability of business units to do what they please is fueled by the technology itself. Cloud computing—renting rather than buying technology—and easily supported devices—such as smartphones and tablets—make it easy for anyone to acquire, deploy and support digital technology. The new cloud-based delivery models and the proliferation of consumerized devices and applications have completely changed the governance game.

Postfederated/Decentralized Technology Adoption and Delivery

Within 5 years, traditional *IT departments* will disappear in many companies. *Technology* will merge with business models and processes, or, more accurately, become seamlessly immersed in business models and processes. The technology function will exist across the businesses fueling numerous business activities and processes—such as sales, marking, finance, customer service, innovation and supply chain management, among the business functions and activities that comprehensively define a company's business models and processes.

In practice, this means that there will be technologists on the business teams. It means that there will be sales technologists, marketing technologists, finance technologists, customer service technologists, innovation technologists and supply chain management technologists—among others who understand both business processes and models and current and emerging digital technologies.

These business technologists will be opportunistic. They will acquire and deploy technology as quickly and cheaply as possible. They will do so because they will be (business unit) *project*—not (enterprise) *standards*—driven. They will be problem solvers working side-by-side with their colleagues in the business functional areas. *Many of them will also work side-by-side with their customers and suppliers, because digital technology—and especially emerging and disruptive technology—is the glue of business.*

Enterprise IT—what we now describe as the keepers of a company's technology infrastructure—will also move. But unlike what we describe today as *business partners*, infrastructure jockeys will move to an enterprise audit. They will pursue a three-pronged agenda: (1) architecture, (2) infrastructure and (3) security. Enterprise IT in corporate audit? It's a natural fit. Audit already owns security and operational performance.

The addition of the architecture function is consistent with audit's role as an optimizing group responsible for making things consistent compliant and measurable. After it moves to audit, enterprise IT—responsible for infrastructure activities such as e-mail, storage, backup and recovery—will do what operational IT does best: deliver secure, recoverable basic services as cheaply as possible. The architectural function is important because it will assure that the technology the lines of business deploy will not crash networks or corrupt infrastructure applications. Audit is the best place to enforce the architectural standards that enterprise IT groups have failed to enforce for decades. Audit is also the best place for another new core competency: cloud and applications service level agreement (SLA) negotiations and management. As procurement is often part of the larger audit team anyway, it's a natural place to locate cloud SLA management.

Agile Technology-Enabled Business Models and Processes

Agile is still all the rage—and why not? Anytime anyone can simultaneously attack a slow/expensive/ineffective process and replace it with a better/cheaper/faster one, there's happiness all the way around. Agile is about the role that technology plays in business problem-solving. Agile is financially unconstrained. Where we previously invested huge amounts of capital in technology assets that locked us into long-term amortization commitments, today we invest operating dollars in technology assets we've never met and to which we have no long-term financial relationship. The whole technology acquisition and deployment process are now fluid, dynamic and unconstrained.

Cloud delivery enables agility, while offering low-cost infrastructure and applications. Low-cost (and sometimes free) applications enable agility. Business technology pilots are not designed to validate discrete requirements, but to discover new continuous ones. If none are discovered you can then move to the next technology-inspired solution. This is agility.

The conventional approach to technology acquisition and design has been replaced by visits to the app store and the cloud. The number of truly new applications design and development projects has fallen dramatically and will continue to fall. The agile-versus-SDLC argument just isn't that relevant anymore.

In the context of organizational change, agile refers to approaches companies adopt to improve technology acquisition and delivery. *We can invest-and-divest in the same day—something that was not conceivable in the twentieth century.* Invest-and-divest agility impacts every aspect of business. Technology-enabled models and processes are quickly discoverable, modifiable, discardable and reconstituteable. The more *agile* the company, the more competitive it is—without the financial drag of old technology acquisition and delivery cycles.

Continuous, Permanent Digital Transformation

The number of *emerging technology vendors* is growing. An increasing number of companies are buying from emerging *and* start-up technology vendors. Emerging technologies are becoming mainstream technologies almost overnight. This is a huge change from the past and directly related to the need for speed and agility. Many *old school* technology buyers and vendors operate within a waterfall procurement process with distinct steps that eventually lead to procurement. The new technology adoption process is much more about speed and relevance—and rapid assessments about the contribution that the technology is (or is not) making to the company.

Companies need speed and agility and the structure of the new marketplace will continue to satisfy these demands. Established technology vendors must adapt to the new technology delivery models even as they struggle with some profit loss: vendors make more money, for example, from licensing enterprise software to their clients versus clients' paying only for what they use. Smaller vendors will attack the markets previously owned by the major established vendors resulting in a much wider set of vendor options for customers seeking fast/cheap/adaptive solutions to their well- *and* ill-defined requirements.

The impact of the new technology marketplace will be profound. It will expand the horizons of the enterprise and business units and enable continuous digital transformation. It will legitimize the inclusion of vendors, products and services that 10 years ago would never have been piloted. The new marketplace will also empower emerging technology vendors who used to think that they had no chance of landing a large account in IBM or HP. But the real impact of the new marketplace will be increased innovation and creativity embedded in ongoing digital transformation projects.

Governance!

Governance is key to technology adoption. Immediate technology adoption assumes federated or decentralized governance. Put another way, it assumes *shared* governance.

Peterson (2004) defines information technology (IT) governance like this:

> IT governance describes the distribution of IT decision-making rights and responsibilities among different stakeholders in the enterprise, and defines the procedures and mechanisms for making and monitoring strategic IT decisions.

In *centralized* technology organizations, decision rights around the acquisition, deployment and support of technology belong to a central group that reports to a corporate executive. In *decentralized* organizations, rights are shared across the enterprise and the business units; and in *federated* organizations, rights are coordinated across the corporate (*enterprise*) IT group, the business units and even in specific corporate functions (Brown and Magill, 1994; Rockart et al., 1996; Weill and Broadbent, 1998; Agarwal and Sambamurthy, 2002; Brown and Grant, 2005; Evaristo et al., 2005; Chan and Reich, 2007; Tiwana et al., 2013; Ullah and Lai, 2013).

Control was the principal driver of governance in the twentieth century. Way back then, overall corporate governance was control-oriented, believing that the more control and standardization, the better. Technology was similarly governed, which is why there was so much of centralized technology governance from 1980 to 2000. But over time, governance began to travel. It moved from centralized to federated structures in which over time business units acquired more and more decision-making power over the acquisition, deployment and support of all digital things.

The changes were driven by several factors, including especially technology consumerization, the widespread availability of outsourcing (especially cloud hosting), the commoditization of technology infrastructure and a constant stream of *ready* technologies (Andriole, 2014a, 2014b). Less centralized governance was also driven by a huge widening of the technology orbit: more and more vendors started playing in the backyards of small, medium and large companies. The *app store* changed everything as more and more technology providers became available—and cheaper. Long-term contracts were replaced by fast-and-cheap demonstration pilots.

Business units were also under extraordinary pressure to generate revenue and profit, especially after the financial meltdown in 2008. To achieve better financial results, business units everywhere demanded more control over the resources necessary to make them successful. As technology became more and more integral to business success, business units demanded control of the digital levers.

By 2000, almost everyone realized that future business processes and models would turn on information technology. This realization meant that companies began searching a long time ago for digital leverage anywhere they could find it. It also meant that the old *command and control* governance models would be challenged every single day—until they all died – by the most conservative companies whose revenue streams were assured by either government subsidies, regulations, or both. These drivers forever changed the way technology was acquired, deployed and supported.

But where will it end?

How far does the governance arm already extend?

Figure 4.1 presents the governance participants (Andriole, 2015). The number of participants in the new governance world has increased, *and nearly all of the growth is outside of the proverbial corporate firewall.*

Some of the new participants have traveled from far away and have reflected the way technology is acquired, deployed and supported, such as the vast number of cloud computing providers that are now under contract. Similarly, integrated supply chains have increased the dependency among many technology providers. Finally, as many customers are glued to their social networks, companies must now engage their customers through communication and content networks that they do not control in any way, shape, or form. *Is the whole concept of technology governance an anachronism?*

Many traditional IT departments will disappear sooner than what we think. *Technology* will seamlessly merge with business

Internal stakeholders			External stakeholders		
The Enterprise	Corporate Functions	Business Units	HW, SW and Service Providers	Partners and Suppliers	The Crowd
The Corporate Entity that Defines the Corporate Mission and the Overarching Reporting Structure of the Organization Including Technology Leaders	Specific Activities that Define Corporate Organizations, Such as Marketing, Finance, Accounting and Human Resources and Information technology	Specific Lines of Business that Focus on Specific Customer Sets with Products and Services that Generate Sales and Profits and That Require Information Technology	Vendors that Provide Hardware, Software, Network and Other services to the Enterprise and Business Units, Increasingly Delivered Via Cloud Service Providers	Business Partners and Suppliers that Enable Business Functions as Well as Product and Service Definition, Manufacturing and Delivery, Among Other Activities	All those Outside of the Enterprise, the Business Units and Providers, Partners and Suppliers Who May Contribute in Any Way to the Success of the Company

Figure 4.1 Governance participants.

models and processes, or, more accurately, become completely immersed in business models and processes. The technology function will exist across the businesses fueling numerous business activities and processes—such as sales, marketing, finance, customer service, innovation and supply chain management, among the business functions and activities that comprehensively define a company's business models and processes. The entire concept of *enterprise IT* will evaporate into the cloud.

This means that there will be *technologists* on all business teams. It means that there will be sales technologists, marketing technologists, finance technologists, customer service technologists, innovation technologists and supply chain management technologists—among others who understand both business processes and models and current and emerging digital technology.

What about the technology professionals who populate this new world? Many of them will immerse themselves in the business units. Others will end up in audit. The skills and competencies going forward will not change as much as *where* they're applied.

Budgeting will follow the lead that federation began. Enterprise budgets for infrastructure, architecture and security will be raised by proportionately billing the business units—who will self-fund their own technology investments.

This new technology world will be quite different from the one with which most of us are familiar. Depending on your perspective, the changes may be revolutionary or evolutionary—or just consistent with twenty-first century business models and processes.

Governance as we've defined it for years, becomes a destination, not a process.

Technology-Driven Opportunities

Companies are now nearly completely dependent on technology for all of their operational and strategic success. This is unprecedented power and influence on technology—which was pronounced irrelevant in 2003 by at least one prominent analyst (Carr, 2003, 2004).

Smartphones, laptops and tablets drive connectivity and transactions, and applications and databases help companies develop, deliver and support new products and services. *The full integration of technology into business models and processes—and vice versa—has occurred.*

Technology today is about opportunities. Some of these opportunities are operational and some are strategic. The list assumes that a great deal of technology has already been commoditized, and that the days of worrying about which laptop to buy, or whether or not to do software upgrade, are behind us. Although companies still buy (or lease) machines and keep software current, these kinds of activities have fully commoditized. Today, the focus is on how technology can help develop new products and services, find and excite customers, and keep communications among employees, customers, suppliers and partners continuous and seamless: IT matters more today than it ever did—and in very different ways than it did a decade ago.

Operational and Strategic Opportunities

There are at least 10 operational and strategic opportunities that define IT today, which is about the exploitation of specific technology capabilities and technology management best practices—*all focused on digital transformation.*

Nearly all of these opportunities are enabled by the quick adoption of emerging technology:

1. Rent as much technology as possible—and eventually almost everything
2. Go as BYOD, thin, mobile—and wearable—as possible
3. Exploit big data analytics
4. Mine social media
5. Keep technology open and agnostic
6. Know where everyone is
7. Track and deploy *ready* technology
8. Crowd source
9. Federate
10. Assess, refresh and relocate technology talent

Rent as Much as Possible—and Eventually Almost Everything

Many of us prefer buying cars to leasing them. We do this because we expect to keep our cars for a very long time and because there's something emotionally pleasing to actually owning the device that powers us along. The interesting thing about cars is that for decades *support* has been outsourced to mechanics and dealers: very few of us actually repair our own cars. So, the buy-versus-lease decision is about expected financial and emotional ROI. Interestingly, however, data suggest that the number of people who lease cars is increasing dramatically. Survey research indicates that those who no longer lease want to be in the replacement car business, they no longer want a special relationship with a car mechanic, and realize that they are very unlikely to keep their cars for 5 years: emotional ROI is impacted by the numbers.

The same trend is occurring with technology. More companies are renting technology than ever before. The cost equation is more than compelling: it's generally far less expensive to rent technology than to buy/install/support technology.

Leasing is also support-free: companies that lease hardware and software are never responsible for fixing anything when it breaks;

they are no longer in the hardware or software business—as many of them have been for decades. The satisfaction with renting is extremely high—more than 90%.

We are within a few years of when companies will lease everything from their cloud providers, including all operational technology—such as e-mail, word processing, spreadsheets, security, database management and enterprise resource planning (ERP)—and strategic technology—such as customer relationship management (CRM), location-based services (LBS), learning management systems (LMS) and predictive analytics. *Many companies are already completely in the clouds.*

One of the major strengths of cloud computing is the freedom it provides companies to think about their business models and processes. Instead of worrying about network latency and server maintenance, companies can focus on innovation, sales and marketing, among other revenue generating activities. Another opportunity is flexibility. Picking from a menu is easier than designing one—and then delivering the food. Scalability is often just a phone call, e-mail, or alert away. The freedom from software maintenance, denial of service attacks, software version control, virus protection, backup and recovery—and other operational headaches is provided by cloud providers.

There's an opportunity to rent hardware, software, storages and services across the board: why would anyone in the twenty-first century buy, install and support an enterprise ERP or database management system? The average cost of an ERP implementation for a Fortune 500 company is $200MM and the probability of failure is well over 50%. The average cost to rent an ERP application is a small fraction of this amount and there is no implementation or support risk; the same reasoning applies to e-mail, storage, security, HR and analytics applications, among just about every activity/application in the modern corporation.

Leasing frees companies to focus on strategies and tactics, not technology. Cloud computing provides the foundation for the adoption of old and new technologies. It also enables agility and competitiveness. Cloud computing also fundamentally alters the technology delivery marketplace and will, ultimately, restructure the entire technology industry.

The opportunities that leasing provides are numerous, ranging from cost savings to new customer acquisition. The ability to exploit cloud computing is a new core competency.

Bring-Your-Own-Device, Thin, Mobile and Wearable

The bring-your-own-device (BYOD) to work delivery model gained momentum immediately after it was described by industry gurus and demonstrated by a few creative companies. As employees have their favorite machines and software applications—and are more productive when they use *personal technology*—and because many companies would love to reduce and eventually eliminate this expensive employee technology benefit, pilots were launched to determine the cost/benefit of BYOD delivery models.

BYOD is now a formal delivery model led by CFOs, CIOs and CEOs that like the idea of letting employees use whatever technology they want—especially if it reduces technology costs. Companies are offering annual stipends to their employees to help reduce the cost of the technology employees prefer. Support is acquired through the vendor of choice. Integration and security are managed through a set of enterprise applications that keep the company's activities operating safely, but otherwise the employee is on his or her own to arrange for support, upgrades and personal digital security.

The objective is the thinnest, most mobile devices possible. Although we still use desktops and laptops, increasingly we have started using tablets, smart phones, and other *thin clients* to access local area networks, wide area networks, virtual private networks and hosted applications on these networks as well as applications that run locally on (some of) the devices. The economics are so compelling for thin clients that we can expect the "fat" corporate PC and even the venerable laptop to slowly disappear from the list of corporate technology assets. BYOD will accelerate this trend.

There's also an opportunity to exploit the capabilities of wearables, such as Apple's *iWatch* and Plantronics' Bluetooth headsets, among countless DIY-enabling devices changing the way we search, navigate, transact and live.

The opportunities go way beyond the technical capabilities of self-selected thin, mobile and wearable devices. Transactions of all kinds are affected by access, location and preference. Business models that accelerate roaming transactions and communications enable continuous business processes, such as Amazon have done so well.

BYOD/thin/wearable/mobile opportunities will improve productivity, fuel agility and geographically distributed business models and processes through technology integration. This means that there are no lines, boundaries, or locations—for customers, suppliers, or employees. It means that companies exist everywhere and that products and services—and innovation and management—are ubiquitous and continuous. The opportunity to extend, widen and deepen business models and processes through BYOD/thin/wearable/mobile technology are only just emerging.

Big (Structured and Unstructured) Data Analytics

The big data analytics opportunity is growing. Data are converting to information as quickly as companies can collect it. While there is an enormous amount of structured and unstructured data flowing into companies, the capacity for analyzing it is also growing proportionately.

But data is no longer owned by the enterprise. It's created by everyone: vendors, customers, suppliers, partners, managers, executives, stakeholders and bloggers, among anyone else that would like to offer insights, solve problems or purchase products and services. Organizing, analyzing and managing all these data are another new core competency.

The strategic goal is real-time descriptive, explanatory, predictive and prescriptive data, information and knowledge about internal and external processes and performance. The torrent of unstructured social media data has overwhelmed conventional collection platforms, though platforms such as Apache's Hadoop/Spark can handle much of the large-scale transaction processing of structured and unstructured data.

Others are working on social media plug-ins to enterprise CRM and ERP platforms.

The power of analytics is clear: the more descriptive, explanatory, predictive and prescriptive insight a company has, the better its operational and strategic performance. The ability to observe and tune operations and strategy—especially in real time—is essential to competitive positioning and growth. Analytics is awareness and engagement. All of this is a huge opportunity for companies of all sizes.

Mine Social Media

A decade ago, some companies actually banned social networks and larger forms of social media. Now all companies are learning to embrace everything social.

Social business intelligence assumes that there's a value in connecting people who are willing or anxious to collaborate through their affinity with friends, colleagues, associates, places, products and brands. Customer service and new product releases are especially vulnerable to twittering. Companies now worry about what's being said about them in social media. There are now any number of companies that help their clients *listen* to what customers, partners and employees are saying about them in Facebook, Twitter, Tumblr, Instagram and TripAdvisor—and countless other social media sites. Some of these companies listen but others extract meaning and purpose from social content—which is what companies really want. Put another way, companies need to not only know *what* people are saying about them, but *why* they're saying and what they're saying—and the response implications of the conversations on products, services and strategies.

The opportunities around social media are extensive. Note that the opportunities include internal and external analyses. While many see social business intelligence as focused primarily on what customers and suppliers are saying, there are opportunities to listen to executives, managers and employees as well. Companies can also just listen or they can socially engage their customers and suppliers.

Keep Technology Open

Distributed architectures, application programming interfaces (APIs) and reusable software components are yielding rapid/active-versus-slow/passive software design. Passive design is what software engineers have practiced for decades: someone identifies *requirements* and then some others code functionality into inflexible software applications.

Everything is fine until a new requirement emerges and changes must be made. Enhanced functionality comes in the form of releases with new features released and supported by the creator of the software— on the creators' schedule.

Instead of rigid embedded process, active software architectures enable the addition or subtraction of functionality through component architectures and APIs that will grow increasingly flexible and available from a variety of sources including the original authors of the software and all kinds of software mercenaries. Open-source APIs will make it possible to reengineer functional designs in near-real-time. Software will be designed in interoperable pieces, not in monolithic structures. APIs and other components will enable functional interoperability, extensibility and adaptability. The integration of disparate cloud delivery technologies is also part of the trend toward architecture compatibility—which is extremely important to the adoption of ready technology.

It's impossible to discuss from where software comes from without examining app stores. The number of applications appearing monthly is staggering. But more significantly, app stores represent a whole new software development and distribution channel. Even more stunning are the prices of the software applications at these stores. Countless robust business-grade applications sell for under $50. Some cost less than $10. What this means for all of us is a whole new way to define software applications and whole new ways to acquire them at unheard of price points—especially given what corporate software buyers expect to pay.

There are countless free open-source software (OSS) applications that are now industry ready and, as data suggest, are industry deployable. Osalt lists the major proprietary software along with open-source alternatives (http://www.osalt.com). It's amazing that how many open-source applications have impressed even the most conservative IT buyers over the past 5 years. OSS is creeping into every layer of the software stack; it's also appearing under its own labels: in which hardly anyone sees *apace*, everyone sees what's happening with Google apps, Google docs, OpenOffice, MySQL, Hadoop/Spark and *SugarCRM* among countless others.

Also note the opportunity to develop new software applications in the cloud. The platform-as-a-service (PaaS) delivery model supports the design, development and deployment (in the cloud, if you must) of new applications that are designed with open flexibility in mind. *Salesforce's Force.com* is an example of PaaS.

Finally, there's the location of the software that we use to enable communication, analysis and transaction processing. Does it sit on your—or your provider's—server? The movement of data center responsibility from internally serviced centers to centers in the cloud describes the journey that software has taken over the decades—not to mention the journey that pricing has taken over the same period. We'll see more pay-by-the-drink pricing models, even if the drink only takes a few minutes—or miliseconds.

The range of opportunities here will keep companies *clean* and *free*. At the heart of the open/agnostic opportunity is the freedom to move data from vendor-to-vendor, the ability to solve problems without expensive proprietary tools and to cost-effectively pivot in the marketplace. For decades, companies were constrained not only by their own organizational problems but also by their technological infrastructures that were proprietary, inflexible and expensive. Open/agnostic technology enables all of this and more.

Know Where Everyone Is

Location awareness fundamentally alters business processes across multiple functional areas, but especially in sales and marketing. Enabled by GPS (and other) technology, retailers can track customers and tempt them with real-time and other offers. But these are only a few of the services that location awareness enables.

The key is to define location-based services and discover the requirements that the technology can satisfy. For example, retailers have a clear vested interest in knowing where their customers physically are. They need to know the movement patterns of their customers and they need to correlate locations with a variety of attributes such as time of day, age, gender, wealth and race, among other variables. The next step is to infer from that data precisely how to engage that customer with just the right communications and offers. Location awareness thus enables customer analytics.

Location-aware platforms enable a variety of activities and transactions and link to other social media sites to enable an *experience* that is both fun and profitable. Companies have developed their own location-aware applications that employees, suppliers and customers can download on to their laptops, smartphones and tablets—to *all* of their mobile devices. As more and more devices (and people) become connected to the Internet—think Internet-of-Things (IoT)—the importance of location awareness only grows.

Historical location data can provide insight into the travels of customers, suppliers, partners and employees. Companies need to prepare for all the primary and secondary transactions that location awareness enables. Again, analytics is one of the capabilities that location awareness enables.

The power of location awareness and location-based services is growing. Location-based services enable the real-time correlation of location-based marketing, selling and service, especially when combined with data about consumer preferences. Companies that touch customers with products and services can avail themselves of location awareness and location-based services—or find themselves at a competitive disadvantage to those who do. The relationship among analytics, social media and location awareness is clear—and cumulative. When integrated with mobility and cloud computing, the potential is even greater.

Companies can exploit opportunities around the collection and analysis of location data in many ways, but especially through the *integration* of location, customer, product, sales and marketing data—all delivered through a public or private cloud.

Track, Pilot and Deploy Emerging Technology

The technology adoption process in the twentieth century was deliberate and careful. Companies subscribed to a requirements-driven process that vetted technologies according to their alignment with known business requirements *and* their operational maturity. The prudent technology adoption model was defined around caution: there were relatively few *early adopters* of business technology in the twentieth century.

The twenty-first century has provided the means to quickly vet and deploy emerging technologies that can *instantly* add business value. Ready technology pilots are as much about solving well-understood business problems as they are about discovering new ones. What was formerly criticized as *solutions in search of problems* can now be embraced as a new technology adoption protocol.

The Wall Street Journal (2012) reports that an increasing number of companies are buying from emerging or even start-up technology vendors. Others report that emerging technologies are becoming mainstream technologies almost overnight. In fact, Currier (2011) reports that drivers of emerging technology adoption include *improving business agility, creating cost savings or productivity enhancements and opening up new markets or opportunities for the enterprise.*

Crowdsource

Expertise was never contained within a corporate firewall. Companies hope to have the best and the brightest way of solving their problems, but there are always other qualified professionals that do not—at the moment—work at a specific company. Today we can look well outside the corporate firewall to *the crowd* for help.

Crowdsourcing is a relatively new problem-solving model. The Internet makes it possible to connect problem creators with problem solvers, instantly and continuously. Small, medium and large companies solve problems alongside *individual contributors* and freelancers. But the definition of *problems* is wide. In fact, there are many crowdsourcing sites that companies can use to solve problems, perform specific tasks and even just brainstorm.

Federate

In the twentieth century, governance was largely about technology standards and centralized control. As we moved into the twenty-first century, things began to change from centralized to federated and control shifted because many of the opportunity areas discussed here, such as BYOD, crowdsourcing, social business intelligence and other *ready* technologies are impossible to centrally control. More importantly, companies realized that trying to control IT all from a single desk made little strategic sense. Although everyone agrees that aspects of operational technology should be centralized, very few companies with multiple lines of business believe that control should include strategic applications that the businesses need to compete (Cloud computing also makes it impossible to control what the business units actually do, because deployment is just a click or phone call away). Within 5 years, technology will merge with business models and processes, or, more accurately, become seamlessly immersed in business models and processes. The technology function will exist across the businesses fueling numerous business activities and processes—such as sales, marketing, finance, customer service, innovation and supply chain management, among all of the business functions and activities that comprehensively define a company's business models and processes.

Assess, Refresh and Relocate Technology Talent

As discussed earlier, many technology professionals will move into business units. Others will move to corporate audit. The skills and competencies going forward will change as much as where they're applied. Although there will always be new skills and competencies—such as cloud SLA design and management—many of the full immersion, softer skills and competencies already exist in business relationship managers. The best infrastructure professionals know how to optimize these basic services—regardless of where they sit. The refresh/relocate opportunity is about the optimization and allocation of talent with expanding skills and competencies.

At least 10 of the above operational and strategic technology opportunities describe the enablers of digital transformation.

The list of opportunities will change over time as will the perspective around the role that IT plays in companies and other organizations. Perhaps the biggest change is the power that IT now has to enable business processes *and* improve profitability. Many of the opportunities will help companies save money and many will help the same companies make money. This is unprecedented—and growing—power and influence for IT: the very thought that "IT Doesn't Matter" (Carr, 2003) is as incomprehensible today as business models that ignore the Internet.

Reality Checks

As we extol the changes underway, it's important to note that not everyone is a champion of technology-driven transformation. Many companies are still resisting the tidal waves that are about to hit their balance sheets (and in some instances, have already devastated their business models).

Every year the *Society for Information Management* (SIM, 2017) publishes the results of their annual survey of what CIOs believe are the most important issues they will face in 2017.

Let's review the 2017 list (based on 2016 survey data) of what keeps CIOs up at night, what the top management issues are and even how CIOs spend their time and then comment on the findings in the context of digital transformation.

Sources of (Temporary) Worry

The overwhelming number of respondents to the SIM survey still live in *completely centralized* or *centralized* houses, where technology is tightly controlled by a small number of people. These modern digital dictators loathe change, which is generally forced on them. They react. They are not proactive change agents or disruptors. How many CIOs do you know who work every day to proactively transform their organizations in response to obvious technology trends and in response to constant calls for digital transformation? How many do you know who enthusiastically share control over the acquisition, deployment and support of technology with the lines of business?

SIM reports that in terms of pure control, respondents overwhelmingly control the technology infrastructure, control the enterprise applications, control IT purchasing and acquisition, control governance and control IT standards setting. Control was shared with the business units only with line of business applications, though more than 50% of the respondents reported that even these applications were *completely centralized* or *centralized.*

Nearly all of the other survey results stem in one way or another from the governance described by the respondents. It's hard to change direction when there's only a tiny management team at the helm—especially when CIOs need all the help they can get to remain relevant and ideally seen as valuable, *cooperative* partners in the business. Industry trends point clearly to shared governance—whether CIOs like it or not (Andriole, 2015).

Most Important Management Concerns

IT departments and managers still worry about alignment with the business, and cybersecurity and innovation top the list. Agility and flexibility are rising slightly in importance, as are business cost controls. Strategic planning is now more important than it was last year, but speed-of-delivery is less important. The SIM survey did not probe deeply about attitudes around digital transformation!

What Keeps Technology Leaders up at Night

There are five worries: (1) cybersecurity, (2) IT talent/skill shortage, (3) alignment of IT with the business, (4) credibility of IT/perception of IT leadership and (5) business continuity.

The alignment problem is so easily solved. Why has it made the list since the 1980s? All CIOs have to do is find out who are their business partners—such as CEOs, COOs and CFOs—think it is important and understand what keeps *them* up at night. Here's a list we found in 3 seconds on *Google*:

1. Regulatory compliance
2. Speed of technological change
3. Taxes and tax policy
4. Social instability
5. Consumer behavior
6. Cyber threats
7. Product and service innovation
8. Competitive advantages
9. Talent retention
10. Mergers & Acquisitions

These lists present clear clues for CIOs and IT managers. "Alignment" is *alignment* with what keeps CEOs, COOs, and CFOs up at night (not what keeps CIOs up night). CIOs should just ask them what keeps them up at night *and then organize, allocate and execute accordingly.*

Where the Money Goes

The list of projects that consume the most cash includes the following: analytics, applications maintenance and development, cybersecurity, cloud computing, CRM, ERP, data centers, application/data integration, networking, legacy applications, disaster recovery, master data management, BPM, innovation with disruptive technologies and staff development and training and retention—in that order.

Spending Trends

Companies are spending less on hardware and software and more on cloud services. The SIM data survey indicates that more companies have increased their technology spending, which is especially evident across distinct industries. Although we applaud increased spending, we're stunned by the rate of growth in technology spending. *Why so low?* Slight increases indicate that investments in digital transformation are lagging. As more and more functional areas—such as finance, marketing, customer service, supply chain management and payment processes, among so many others—go digital, why would n't technology budgets rise more aggressively (as functional budgets fall proportionately)? The best spending metric is not technology spending as a percentage of revenue or even spending as a percentage of specific industries. *The best metric is technology spending across functional areas that indicates an organization's commitment to leveraging the right technology at the right time.* Such metrics would reveal—ideally—that companies are, for example, spending more and more on digital marketing, more on automated customer service and more on intelligent systems to manage and optimize the customer journey.

A surprising SIM finding is the persistence of investments in software development and maintenance, *which still consume almost 25% of the budget.* This metric suggests—because of its multiyear persistence—that efforts to decommission legacy applications are failing. Investments in new applications (not integration) should also always be rigorously questioned in which cloud-delivered packaged applications being the rule, not the exception. When the software budget is decomposed, SIM survey respondents reported that a whopping 50% of the software cash goes to legacy maintenance and enhancement, 45% goes to *customization* and 27% goes to completely new application development. This finding alone explains the popularity of digital transformation.

More People (But Less Security)

Given the acquisition, deployment and support options we have today—think cloud—why is the number of employees rising? Worse, how in the world is the industry's *involuntary turnover* rate only 2.7%? Given the pace of technology change, radically different technology delivery models, architectural shifts and the need for better and deeper soft skills, should we assume that the vast majority of technology employees are *current*, understand emerging digital architectures, cloud optimization and have superior communication and negotiation skills and competencies? These numbers reflect a ton of resistance to change. Much worse, the survey data suggest that relatively few technology professionals plan to retire!

Great—and not surprising—news about the cloud, however. Increased cloud delivery is skyrocketing—though legacy applications continue to terrorize too many companies. But why are so many companies opposed to charge-back accounting for technology services when cloud delivery enables metering? Cloud delivery is the path to pay-by-the-drink models that federate cost controls to the line of business.

Incredibly, 54% of the companies who responded to the SIM survey have no chief information security officer (CISO).

Chief Information Officers Lifestyle

CIOs are apparently living longer than they did a few years ago. Most survive for 5 corporate years. It is impressive, though retail cashiers usually last longer. CIOs also mostly report to CEOs (46%), though a healthy percentage (28%) report to the CFO. While we prefer line of business CIOs who report to their line of business (LOB) presidents, the SIM survey was largely completed by very tightly governed organizations.

We're struck by the increasing amount of time that CIOs report they spend alone—13%—which is more time than CIOs spend with contractors, vendors, external customers, suppliers, or outside technology colleagues. It's also close to the percentage of time they spend on *non-IT, non-C-level employees* in their companies (17%). Why do CIOs spend so much time alone? Even more startling is the percentage of time CIOs spend with internal business clients (27%) versus the percentage of time (63%) they spend on *IT-related* activities. CIOs should live with the business, not in the IT bunkers—even if they're highly centralized—and especially if they want to enable digital transformation.

From Therapy to Adoption to Transformation

The SIM survey results describe the twentieth century almost perfectly. Traditional *IT* needs to radically change its focus and structure. Legacy applications must disappear into packaged applications in the cloud. Digital security is the new, permanent high priority investment target: CISOs everywhere, all the time. Companies should double down on cloud delivery. Talent should be continuously assessed. Companies should resist new development and reduce the size of their teams, which should distribute into businesses as healthy transformation viruses. Federated governance will accelerate. But most of all, CIOs should stop worrying about what they can control. Digital transformation is about less—not more—governance.

The Technology-Driven Enterprise

As IT organizations change, technology adoption accelerates and technology acceleration enables digital transformation. The SIM survey data mark a point in time that describes the last gasp of twentieth century organization, structure and governance. It's described here for purpose. Twenty-first century technology organizations will respond almost completely differently than their twentieth century predecessors. Perhaps the best way to understand where we're going is to fully expose where we've been.

Our data conflicts with SIM data in some important aspects: our survey polled IT professionals, business managers, executives and other functional professionals; the SIM survey polled SIM members—many of which are CIOs. Is there a lesson here?

5

Forward Guidance

Our research suggests that emerging and disruptive technology is now perceived as a digital weapon. It's therefore often immediately piloted and quickly deployed by companies that want to improve their competitiveness through digital transformation.

We learned that digital transformation relies on the rapid adoption of emerging and sometimes disruptive technology.

Obviously *digital* transformation assumes the optimization of *digital technology*, but before companies cherry-pick technologies from pundit-pruned lists, they must conceptually understand what the technologies do and the degree of possible optimization-through-transformation. *In other words, digital transformation is most effective when there's an objective and where baskets of technologies are hypothetically linked to the objectives. As discussed, this means that digital transformation is most effective when it's semifocused—which is a departure from the requirements-first/technology-second approach practiced in the twentieth century.*

Enterprise IT—the organization and management of corporate-wide technology acquisition and management in a single enterprise office—*are dead.* The whole concept of one-size-fits-all or, worse, the idea that the *people-in-corporate* understand what business units need to compete is flat-out wrong. Technology-enabled business models and processes are free agents, not subservient to bureaucrats who report to the corporate establishment. *The death march actually began in the late twentieth century—just about the time when technology adoption processes began to change. The death march began when technology federated to business units.*

Many enterprise CIOs, CTOs, CFOs and even CEOs are tone deaf to the technology tornados around them. There's a huge disconnect between corporate ascendency and technology trajectories. Put another way, technology moves faster than executives can climb the corporate ladder. So, by the time they get to the top, the technologies they're expected to optimize are as strange to them as the ten-mile run they used to do every day, so many decades ago. The rules that made them *Chiefs* have also changed, even if they don't always see IT that way.

This disconnect is lethal to digital transformation (though it's rapidly disappearing). Some of the very same chiefs often need courses in technology postmodernism and especially technology management just to communicate with their internal clients—who are now real *clients*, not *subjects*. Many of them still believe in standardization, centralized governance, TCO, internal software development and the SDLC. *These Chiefs are not the champions of immediate technology adoption or are likely to lead digital transformation projects.*

But their clients—and replacements—are.

Many have no idea how the business units see *participatory governance* or *digital transformation*. Exhausted from the climb, many CIOs and CTOs have no energy for personal or professional transformations. Instead, they try to wait it out, to just get out before the other shoe falls. As they leave, one by one, technology adoption accelerates and prospects for successful digital transformation skyrocket.

What's Happening?

Here are the overall trends:

- The whole notion of enterprise IT as an organizational asset is dying—except for the asset that delivers basic computing and communications services (most of which are already cloud-based commodities and therefore already out the door).
- Business units chase new strategic technologies that make them more profitable as voraciously as technologies will pursue—and redefine—new business models and processes: technology adoption happens here ... disruption happens here ... ROI is calculated here—not at the enterprise level.

- Business units couldn't care less about basic infrastructure services: they just want everything to work … they want to control the technology that keeps them competitive.
- The retreat from monster enterprise applications such as ERP and enterprise DBMS platforms that must be sold to everyone (to justify the staggering cost of monolithic applications and platforms) continues: one size never fits all—and in the early twenty-first century (and forever), it seldom fits anyone.
- Companies already drunk with enterprise ERP and DBMS applications and platforms are beginning the full migration to cloud-based enterprise applications where they can rent their way out over time: think of the migration process as parole when as companies plan for freedom.
- Concepts such as enterprise governance and standardization are already Old Testament and resurrecting them will only keep IT in the desert: companies are learning how to read the gospel from the business pulpit, not the technology trenches.
- The future is an unmanaged free-for-all: whatever remains of traditional *IT* will focus exclusively on keeping the lights on, which IT will do with a suite of cloud providers that IT will manage … beyond operational technology, business units will determine what technology they need, when they need IT and what they're willing to pay to rent IT: CAPEX is dead … long live OPEX.
- Immediate technology adoption will occur in the business units much more frequently than the enterprise.

These trends challenge technology management and especially technology optimization on every level. Although many companies assume that the chief-is-dead, many others are still fighting the trends flying away from standardization, centralized governance, TCO, internal software development, the SDLC, phased technology adoption and technology pilots that last for years versus months or even weeks. They refuse to see technology as holistic, shared and uncontrollable. They still want to govern IT (as if they ever really did, ignoring *Shadow IT* spending that's been rising for decades). Our data indicate that the concept of control is obsolete.

Enterprise IT Is Dying

If the list below were rank ordered, each item would be a *10*. IT is changing so quickly and thoroughly because it's being *simultaneously* challenged by at least seven macrotrends:

- Demographics are killing IT
- Consumerization is diluting IT
- Globalization is spreading IT
- New business processes are crushing IT
- Vendors are confusing—and forcing—IT
- Business units are leaving the building
- One-size-fits-all is inconsistent with innovation on every level

Millennials and generations Y and Z do not see technology at all the way baby boomers see IT. The challenge of course is that many chiefs are boomers or *old* millennials who see technology as tools or at best transaction enablers, not as the essence of business models, processes and purposes. They see corporate *strategy* at the center of business functions, while *technology* has already displaced strategy's central role in the overall business process.

Consumerization is now the driving force of corporate technology awareness, as the distance between *personal* and *professional* computing shrinks.

Let's also not forget that technology is now everywhere, all the time. But even more importantly, what we expect from technology is now *comprehensive transaction processing* that enables current, emerging *and unpredictable* business models and processes. The gang of vendors surrounding all this change is driving technology pervasiveness—for obvious financial reasons—as they create, deploy and support technology in always-on clouds that permit companies to try-before-they-buy *and deploy the next day*. Regardless of these drivers of change are business units that are simply leaving the building, going their own technology way. Shadow IT—along with immediate technology adoption—is now a way of life. Profit-generating business unit presidents don't even hide IT anymore. Finally, how does any monolithic approach to technology—unless it's restricted to infrastructure technology—enable innovation? *The relationship between monolithic IT and innovation is an impossible abstraction—and nothing more.*

Birth of Digital

So what should CIOs, CTOs, CFOs and CEOs do?

- Laser-seek the centers of corporate power ... locate the business unit that generates the most revenue and profit—and therefore the most personal wealth for the senior management team (SMT) ... befriend these people (especially the profitable BU presidents)—even if they're hateful and the biggest shadow IT spenders in the company: they are the new digital power centers and CIOs' new best friends—or worst powerful enemies.
- Discover and build new core competencies, including BPM, digital security, competitive analysis, disruptive business technologies, demos, executive briefings and personality, because CIOs, CTOs and even architects are now—actually always were—politicians.
- Absolutely and finally separate infrastructure from everything else—and then give IT away: IT's time, way past time.
- Go with the trends and stop fighting what cannot be controlled (even if you're close to retirement) ... embrace and accelerate the trends ... never, ever be perceived as begrudgingly acceptance of trends everyone believes you hate.
- Price digital technology on a pay-by-the-drink basis: those who use the most infrastructure technology should pay the most; business units should pay for their own strategic technology.
- Publically rebrand technology around the themes of transformation, competitiveness and profitability—never governance, standardization, TCO, or control.
- Objectively assess your (and your entire team's) ability to enthusiastically endorse and propel digital transformation—and do IT from the outside in: ask your vendors, consultants and especially your business partners if they see digital in you and your team ... respond accordingly—and quickly.

Digital transformation lives at the intersection of technology trends, business processes and competition. The new competencies of disruptive business technologies, business process modeling (BPM), and competitiveness analysis are essential to the digital transformation. If companies shortchange any of them, their transformation efforts will fail. There is no substitute for understanding business processes and models, and the models and processes of the competition. Subject matter expertise never dies and is now more important than ever. How else can the *right* digital technology be selected and leveraged?

The role that digital security plays in the digital transformation is undeniable and growing. CIOs should work with the business units and corporate audit to keep everyone safe.

It's also important to recognize the role that soft skills play in digital transformation. As governance is becoming increasingly distributed and shared, the need for communication, persuasion, trust and negotiation—among other skills—is spiking.

Demonstrations (followed by rapid pilots) are the weapons of modern corporate warfare. CIOs and CTOs must organize demo factories capable of testing new technologies in a matter of weeks. They must also be able to communicate test results with charts, graphs and terms that are meaningful to their internal business clients.

Digital Transformation Skills and Competencies

Business is changing but the ability to respond to shifting markets, demographics and aggressive competitors is constrained often because companies are not properly leveraging current, emerging and even potentially disruptive digital technology. So, their digital transformation projects are failing—and will continue to fail until they master the 15 technologies, best practices and soft skills described here.

If they've underinvested in these technologies, best practices and soft skills they will fail. Put another way, if they're overinvested in enterprise software development, help desk management and in-house applications support they've undermined their digital transformation possibilities. Remember, the role of *technology* has changed. The chances are good that a company's business-technology strategy is optimized for the twentieth century. *But today the successful technology organization is a management organization, not a development organization. It does not create. It applies, exploits and optimizes.*

There are at least 15 technologies, best practices and soft skills that are necessary to optimize the new business–technology relationship in the twenty-first century. They can be organized in three baskets: (1) technologies, (2) business–technology management best practices and (3) soft skills. If companies want to transform their business with current, emerging, or disruptive digital technology, they need to invest in all 15.

The list below actually presents *the short list* of must-have capabilities (the defined list appears as follows):

1. *Cloud computing*: As everything is moving to the cloud
2. *Analytics*: As descriptive, explanatory and predictive insight is transactional lifeblood
3. *Digital security*: As digital transformation can be derailed by data breaches
4. *Digital media*: As all content is digital, especially social content
5. *Emerging technologies*: As your next disruptive technology is already here!
6. *Project and program management*: Since you must know how to size, scope and watch
7. *Vendor management*: As Request for Proposal (RFPs) and Service Level Ageements (SLAs) are now a way of life
8. *Digital security management*: As security vendors and auditors are your new best friends
9. *Business analysis*: As requirements always change and *the business* is tech's only client
10. *Metrics*: As everyone needs to measure—and know—everything.
11. *Written communications skills*: As you need to write clearly and purposefully
12. *Verbal communications skills*: As they will listen if you're coherent-with-style
13. *Collaboration skills*: As no techman or techwoman is an island
14. *Persuasion and negotiation skills*: As everyone disagrees until persuaded otherwise
15. *External presentation skills*: As techies need to be housebroken before leaving the office

Digital Transformation Readiness

Figure 5.1 describes five steps companies should take to assess their transformation readiness. Digital transformation projects include those projects that represent change through the application of existing, emerging and disruptive technology. They include improvements to customer acquisition processes, customer service, supply chain planning, digital media integration, analytics-driven management, and location-based services, among other business processes that might be transformed with digital emerging or disruptive technology. Emerging and disruptive technologies enable transformation, such as the use of augmented reality to improve education and learning, the use of location-based services for real-time cross-selling and upselling and the application of automated reasoning to transaction processing.

Best practices *enable* the optimization of digital transformation; the right soft skills *sustain* digital transformation.

Skills and Competencies for Digital Transformation

The 15 technologies, best practices and soft skills necessary for successful digital transformation are defined in detail here (Andriole, 2017b).

The first set is about technologies:

1. *Cloud computing*: The focus here is on knowledge of, and experience with, all flavors of cloud computing, including all of the service models that cloud computing provides such as

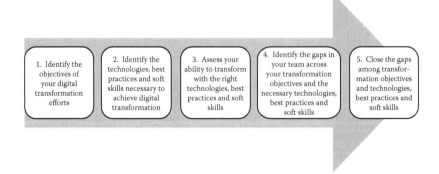

Figure 5.1   Transformation readiness steps.

infrastructure-as-a-service (IaaS), software-as-a-service (SaaS), platform-as-a-service (PaaS), security-as-a-service (SaaS), mobility-as-a-service (MaaS), analytics-as-a-service (AaaS) and even learning-as-a-service (LaaS). It's also about knowledge of, and experience with, alternative cloud delivery architectures, cloud service level agreements (CSLAs), cloud performance metrics and cloud virtualization (especially container) technologies.

2. *Analytics*: The focus here is on knowledge of, and experience with, structured and unstructured descriptive, explanatory and predictive analytics. It also includes knowledge of, and experience with, the major open source analytics platforms such as Hadoop and Spark, among others. It focuses on data science, data representation, deep learning, simulation and displays.

3. *Digital security*: The focus here is on knowledge of, and experience with, the variety of current and emerging security technologies, including technologies such as blockchain technology, multifactor authentication, application isolation, intelligent/automated security tools, mobile application wrapper technology, detection technologies, IaaS/SaaS device security technologies, automated testing and pervasive/IoT security technologies, among others.

4. *Digital media*: The focus here is on knowledge of, and experience with, all forms of digital media especially social media. As Wikipedia describes:

> Digital media can be created, viewed, distributed, modified and preserved on digital electronic devices. Computer programs and software; digital imagery, digital video; video games; web pages and websites, including social media; data and databases; digital audio, such as mp3s; and eBooks are examples of digital media … combined with the Internet and personal computing, digital media has caused disruption in publishing, journalism, entertainment, education, commerce and politics.

5. *Emerging technologies, especially potentially disruptive technologies*: The focus here is on knowledge of, and experience with, emerging technologies that might disrupt the business

rules, processes and models of specific vertical industries and companies. The focus assumes competency in competitive technology intelligence. It also assumes wide and deep knowledge of, and experience with, the adoption of disruptive technology. Of special importance are emerging/disruptive technologies such as virtual/augmented reality, automated reasoning, cashless payment systems, real-time analytics, e-Book technology, simulation/gaming technology, location-based technology and disruptive interface technologies such as intelligent speech, among others.

Best practices are also grouped into five areas and are defined as follows:

6. *Project and program management*: The focus here is on knowledge of, and experience with, project and program management tools, techniques and best practices. It assumes knowledge of, and experience with, project and program management of small and large-scale technology projects and familiarity with the array of tools available to professional project and program managers. This assumes the ability to manage projects and programs cost-effectively and within task-defined timelines. Project and program managers should be professionally certified (by organizations such as the Project Management Institute [PMI]).

7. *Vendor management*: The focus here is on knowledge of, and experience with, technology vendor management best practices. This assumes knowledge of, and experience with, the development of requests for information (RFIs), requests for proposals (RFPs) and requests for quotes (RFQs), including automated tools to develop and compare these documents. This also assumes the development of detailed service level agreements (SLAs) and management tools for measuring SLA compliance. Communications and negotiation skills are also part of this management area. Finally, it's essential to demonstrate knowledge of, and experience with, RFI/RFQ/RFP/SLA-based cloud vendor management.

8. *Digital security management*: The focus here is on knowledge of, and experience with, security challenges and processes, including security policies and the adoption of best practices,

compliance with industry standards (such as ISO27002), regulatory compliance across the entire university, vulnerability assessment/remediation, penetration testing, incident response, network and systems monitoring, forensic analysis, security awareness and training, backup and recovery, among others. The focus should be on audit-approved security-as-a-service, not on in-house security delivery core competencies.

9. *Business analysis*: The focus here is on knowledge of, and experience with, BPM, requirements identification, modeling and validation and digital transformation. It also assumes the ability to model existing and future business processes and whole new business models, ideally within BPM tool sets. This area also assumes knowledge of, and experience with, requirements matching with external vendor capabilities and specific transformation programs and projects.

10. *Metrics*: The focus here is on knowledge of, and experience with, operational, delivery, organization and financial metrics, including metrics around online cloud application performance, cloud application availability, delivery incidents, SLA adherence, project performance (especially satisfaction), personnel performance reviews, budgeting and resource costs. Knowledge and experience here also refers to the tools available to track, measure and report technology performance metrics.

Finally, there are five necessary *soft skill sets*:

11. *Written communications skills*: The focus here is on experience writing reports and creating presentations that are easily understood and therefore actionable. The key to communication is purposeful brevity: is the team capable of such (written) communication? Written communications skills should also be customized to specific audiences, such as executives, boards, internal auditors, sales and marketing professionals and customers, among others.

12. *Verbal communications skills*: The focus here is on experience making presentations that are easily understood and therefore actionable. The key to verbal communications is also purposeful brevity: is the team capable of such (verbal) communication? Verbal communications skills should also be customized

to specific audiences, such as executives, boards, internal auditors, sales and marketing professionals and customers, among others.

13. *Collaboration skills*: The focus here is on the ability to work productively with teams of all shapes and sizes. This ability requires experience and *soft* skills that integrate and optimize team contributions.

14. *Persuasion and negotiation skills*: The focus here is on the ability to persuade and negotiate in a zero-sum world. The most obvious capability here is with internal constituencies regarding budgeting. But the capability includes project prioritization and inter- and intragroup leadership.

15. *External presentation skills*: The focus here is on experience in presenting to outside constituencies and stakeholders, especially vendors, external auditors, customers and professional organizations. Senior members of the technology team must be *presentable* to a wider external audience. As the company's business–technology representatives—and as one of the principal spokespersons for digital transformation—the senior technology team (especially the CIO, CTO and CISO) must all be superb presenters.

These 15 technologies, best practices and soft skills should be used to assess digital transformation capabilities, which involve *objective* workforce assessment of the business–technology team. If gaps exist—*as they likely will*—companies must react accordingly.

Filling the Gaps

Digital transformation is complicated yet potentially extremely impactful, especially when transformation leverages emerging and disruptive technology.

There are three options: (1) repair, (2) rent, or (3) replace.

The repair option is often a good one: retrain and retool the willing keepers. Rethink how many full-time permanent technology professionals are necessary: *rent the others as consultants, contractors and long-term vendors.*

Unfortunately, companies may also have to replace some members of the business–technology team. Although this is always difficult, it's also expensive to keep the unsalvageables. The unsalvageables will also threaten competitiveness.

Digital transformation is challenging but continuously necessary. This is not the first time we've heeded the call to *reengineer* and it won't be the last. *Digital transformation* is today's unique call to action. It's *unique* today because of the trajectory of digital technology and the impact that current, emerging and disruptive technology has had on business processes and whole new business models. Industries and companies now live in fear of disruption because of what's happened to the travel, delivery, transportation, insurance and retail industries. The real estate, banking and election industries are next—and with a vengeance. Said differently, if a company is not a disrupter, it's disruptable. Digital transformation thus becomes a survival tactic *and* a long-term strategy.

So where do we go from here?

Good Technology Clusters

There are at least five technology clusters that enable digital transformation. The (in 2017) clusters appear in the following sections. Note the symbol $: the more, the better (Figure 5.2).

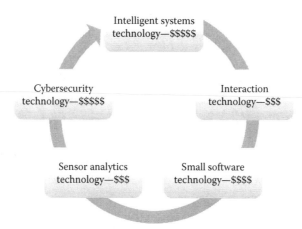

Figure 5.2 Good technology clusters.

Intelligent Systems Technology

Artificial intelligence (AI) is now embedded in a wide array of software applications, infrastructures, business rules, processes and even whole business models. IBM's *Watson* is the face of the popular media's *AI*, but intelligent systems technology encompasses so much more, including deductive and inductive inference, deep learning, machine learning and the tools and techniques used to represent and process data, information and knowledge (such as neural network modeling) as well as the applications of the technology to a host of problems such as conversational speech, language translation, predictive analytics, diagnostics, autonomous vehicles, network management, weapons systems and augmented and virtual reality, among so many other applications that will affect us all.

The development, embedding and application of intelligent systems technology are accelerating and will continue to do so in 2017 and well beyond.

Interaction Technology

The way we interact with all things digital—and physical—is changing. We see and experience content virtually and through augmented reality. We use wearables to track ourselves, our heath, our friends, our transactions and just about everything else we do, see and hear. We allow location-based services to track us around and we buy just about everything with applications on mobile devices. We converse with knowledge bases with relatively crude tools such as *Siri, Alexa and Google Home*, but within a few years we'll be having *meaningful* conversations with increasingly intelligent assistants and—eventually—managers. In addition to voice interaction, we're well on the way to gesture and other controls that mimic the way we interact with humans. Most of this is offered—not created—by users, but companies will avail themselves of the emerging and disruptive interaction technology that can improve productivity and cost-effectiveness.

Small Software Technology

Small software delivered from the cloud is a major technology cluster. The age of monster software applications—such as huge multimodule enterprise resource planning (ERP) applications—is over. Software is decoupling and shrinking. Even software that (stubbornly) hasn't decoupled (yet) is offered in pieces from the cloud to clients who can select the modules they need—and ignore the ones they don't. For those who want newer, smaller and cheaper packages, there are software vendors such as *Zoho* and *Zendesk* who have reduced functionality to its most diagnostic properties. The small software technology cluster will grow until software becomes Lego-like that can be assembled and disassembled at will. As the open-source application programming interface (API) world expands, small software technology will grow. The key trend here is the under-reliance on large integrated software applications and the adoption of smaller, more focused applications accessible on every screen (and from every voice) we have. Investors can exploit this trend (and perhaps make some additional money by shorting some of the software giants).

Sensor Analytics Technology

Ubiquitous sensors capable of tracking, analyzing and predicting all sorts of activities will soon connect everything. The Internet-of-Things (IoT) and then the Internet-of-Everything (IoE) will generate enormous real-time data/information/knowledge streams that must be managed and optimized. The ubiquity of sensors will change today's understanding of *analytics*. The deployment of sensors should be tracked as assiduously as we track advances in data science and analytics. The more sensors, the greater the analytical requirements and the greater will be the number of predictive and prescriptive opportunities. Companies should invest in expanded analytics with the assumption that data, information and knowledge will be continuously exploding and that *analytics* as we practice it today will disappear. It will be replaced by a larger, smarter integration across multiple technology clusters.

Cyber Security Technology

All of the technology clusters underscore the importance of digital security. There's the *business* of security—audits, compliance, policies and procedures—and the *security technology* itself.

The business side lags the technology side (which lags the device and applications sides). All security architectures must continuously adapt while recognizing that the security industry is essentially a reactive one destined to chase solutions to problems it had no idea existed an hour, a day, or a week ago. Several of the enabling technologies include the broad blockchain family. Although blockchain and similar technologies are here to stay, issues such as centralized versus distributed integration and legacy architecture compatibility will persist. There will be significant required cooperation among implementation parties for blockchain to become core to many flavors of transaction processing (beyond cryptocurrency). The business challenge for blockchain companies will be *market share*: will it be open and diffuse (*neutral*) or aggressively proprietary and *closed*. The cybersecurity technology cluster requires continuous attention, investment, testing and implementation within an array of clusters, including *and beyond* those discussed here. In fact, the cybersecurity technology cluster is the most interconnected cluster discussed here.

The clusters presented here exist in an endless world of interdependencies. The arrow that connects the clusters in Figure 5.2 is extremely understated in its importance. Not only do the clusters build on each other, they also depend on each other for implementation. For example, sensor analytics technology assumes the existence of massive amounts of real-time streaming sensor data and some intelligent processing as well as cybersecurity technology to keep it all secure. Similarly, small software technology requires advanced interaction technology to deliver functionality to consumer and corporate clients. There are also numerous technology standards around sensor interfaces and open APIs that will accelerate the adoption of disruptive technologies. The discussion around clusters here assumes that these (and other) standards will evolve.

There's at least one more investment opportunity: technology integrators. As always, technology integrators will benefit from the interdependencies among the technology clusters, so there may be some good opportunities in consultancies that understand technology clusters and how they work together. Companies that make it all work will do very well—assuming they have the necessary breadth and depth among the clusters to succeed.

Bad Technology Clusters

We looked at the technology clusters that will *enable digital transformation*. We discussed intelligent systems technology, interaction technology, small software technology, sensor analytics technology and cybersecurity technology. We identified these five as technology clusters that will enable the success of digital transformation projects. Although we're not clairvoyant, we suggested—based on technology trends research we conduct on an ongoing basis—some technology clusters that should yield solid returns over time. But the same research suggests there are some areas that will not enable impactful digital transformation. Said differently, there are baskets of technologies that will not likely yield *differentiated* digital transformation.

As suggested in Figure 5.3, there are at least five clusters that fall into this category.

Very Big Software

As we've said, *who in their right mind would undertake a five-year ERP software implementation project? Depending on whose study you read, the ERP failure rate is anywhere between 50% and 75%* (Standish Group, 2015). Big software from vendors such as SAP, Oracle, Salesforce, Microsoft and IBM may well see their enterprise software business units shrink. This is because of the changing business processes, cloud

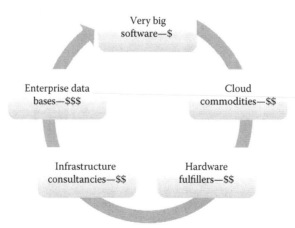

Figure 5.3 *Bad* technology clusters.

delivery, cost, complexity, governance and the constant need to digitally transform old business rules, processes and models. There's also the competition: companies can find lots of incredibly inexpensive alternatives from vendors such as *Zoho* and *Zendesk*, among many others. Many of these companies will grow—as will the incredibly inexpensive, cloud-based systems that scale and integrate right along with them. For big software vendors to survive, they must radically change their offerings, service models and software architectures (from monolithic to microservices-based) delivery strategies—and the management of all of the aforementioned as they turn their aircraft carriers around. Can they do it? Regardless, *monolithic architectures constrain digital transformation.*

Cloud Commodities

How many cloud providers can there be? Initially, the world was introduced to a handful of what we called *application service providers*, or ASPs. These were the trailblazers. Over time, cloud hosting and delivery from start-ups began to change the industry. Then the largest vendors began offering cloud services until—to close the loop—even the major software vendors became cloud providers. In the beginning, cloud vendors were mainly software-as-a-service (SaaS) providers, but in a relatively short period of time IaaS joined the repertoire. Now anyone can rent anything from the cloud. The trend is clear: cloud delivery adoption rates have sky-rocketed. CIOs just assume that applications, infrastructure and services will be cloud-based. Cloud delivery is commoditizing and the competitive advantages around cloud delivery are shrinking. Cloud vendor prices will therefore decrease as services increase. Partnerships between software vendors and cloud providers will also change as more and more applications and infrastructure services blur into integrated service models and container technology will reduce client loyalties. Commoditization, integration and blurring will all challenge cloud delivery as a digital transformation differentiator.

Hardware Fulfillers

The hardware industry comes in two forms: (1) consumer products and (2) consumer/business components. This is the classic razor versus razor blade business model. The consumer hardware space will continue to be brutally competitive along two vectors: (1) coolness and (2) cost. The battle for coolness—such as the battle between *Apple* (*Macs; iPads*) and *Microsoft* (*Surfaces*)—will be decided by consumers voting with their money and ultimately by how innovative vendors are. Competition here will remain brutal across the consumer and professional markets. Scale will be increasingly defined around cost and coolness, but scale threatens profitability simply because the competition is so brutal. Exceptions, of course, include truly disruptive hardware (with innovative software) like what the *iPod* did for the music industry. But these disruption events have become few and far between as more and more vendors race to the profitable bottom of new markets, like what happened to the smart watch and larger wearable product markets. The good news is that all of these consumer and business products rely on computing and communications hardware. Digital transformers can expect fierce competition in the hardware cluster, but there's not a lot of competitive advantages to be found in hardware: everyone can buy the same toys.

Infrastructure Consultancies

In the twentieth century, many companies relied on *IT services* companies to define, deploy and support their computing and communications infrastructures. These vendors made fortunes running data centers, architecting networks, building database management platforms, selling servers and even *fixing* broken devices. They sold infrastructure management software as well. But consultancies who believe that infrastructure service is still a good business model will continue to lose market share to small software vendors, cloud infrastructure providers and consumerized solutions that used to be *centralized* in *enterprises*. Consultancies that fail to morph into cloud/analytics/ intelligent device providers will continue to lose market share. Look no further than the old versus yet-to-be *new* IBM (Andriole, 2015). Older consultancies have a much more difficult time morphing than newer ones. Digital transformers can enlist any number of infrastructure support teams to achieve results. Infrastructure services—such as cloud services—are commodities. Although they must be leveraged carefully, they will not generally transform business rules, processes, or models.

Enterprise Data Bases

Remember when huge database management systems from IBM, Microsoft and Oracle ruled the digital world? Most of you probably don't because you're not that familiar with the twentieth century. But there was a time when the big three owned DBMS. Things are different now. Data is now distributed and unstructured, and while the old/new DBMSs can handle structured and unstructured data analytics, some companies are not as facile with unstructured data analytics, especially real-time unstructured data analytics as some of their younger competitors who rely on open source software like Hadoop. There's also the location of data, which is becoming increasingly cross-located, shared and even co-owned. Sensor-generated data will trigger new collection, cleansing, storage and processing methods and tools and techniques, which is why some of the larger vendors are snapping up IoT start-ups. As the old/new DBMS vendors try to cope with big data requirements, they will quickly find that enterprise-wide solutions will likely to fail. Even more threatening for traditional vendors is the (digital) intelligence that will extend the meaningfulness of *data*, which will become most valuable through inferences made about pieces—not whole databases kept in data centers under lock and key. Digital transformers should partner with data/information/knowledge→analytics vendors that treat big data differently from the old big three.

There are, however, several problems with lists similar to these. First, they're never exhaustive. They're also presented at high levels of abstraction. At the same time, they help us break free of bounded definitions of technologies that appear on everyone's *top 10* lists. The *good* and *evil* clusters discussed here are intended to change everyone's perspective on emerging and disruptive technologies from definitions and descriptions of individual technologies to how technologies form clusters that exist in an endless world of interdependencies. This perspective should change the way companies invest in emerging and disruptive technologies for digital transformation. It suggests that companies should step back from specific investments in individual technologies and invest in multiple technology clusters. It further suggests that those who champion specific technologies—such as *AI*, wearables and big data analytics—rethink their dedication to small baskets of technologies and think about whole clusters of technologies and how the clusters are greater than the sum of their parts.

Transformation-Ready Industries

But what about old→new industries? Where are the opportunities for transformation the greatest? Where emerging/disruptive technologies should be immediately adopted? Here are five industries ready for transformation—five industries in the *technology kill zone.*

If your company is in one of the five industries discussed here, you already know you're in the kill zone. You know that technology will eventually maim and kill your industry though you may be in denial, just like the book, CD, music and taxi industries were in denial until their death (though they had to know deep down that death was inevitable). Protecting revenue streams—even if they're dying—is a form of dystopian art that's well practiced by those who manage the death of business models for a living. But eventually the revenue streams end and the business model dies.

So here are some questions about what's coming next:

1. Why are there insurance agents?
2. What value do realtors actually provide?
3. Why are there banks with drive-in tellers who actually exchange physical *money*?
4. Why are there still so many organic professionals?
5. Why are political elections physical?

Insurance

The insurance industry has already been attacked by digital agents, but the digital army is now poised for a takeover. Most millennials do not use home, auto and life insurance agents. In fact, around 67% of millennials purchase insurance directly from insurance companies and bypass *agents* altogether.

Why in the world would anyone with a computer or smartphone make an appointment with a human being and physically travel to an office? As IBM (2016) reminds us, it's worse:

So, how are millennials shopping for insurance? Online! A little over half of UK millennials say that "comparison web sites" most influence their insurance buying decisions, while just under half say that "searching online" does. And, don't be surprised when online research doesn't include your website—at least, not at first. Millennials overwhelmingly don't trust insurance companies. An IBM Institute for Business Value survey reports that, "89% of millennial consumers believe friends' comments more than company claims," and "93% of millennial consumers usually read reviews before making a purchase."

Agents are paid conduits for insurance companies who use them as sales channels. They're willing to compensate agents who bring them business, but as buying patterns change, the value agents bring to insurance carriers will fall. More importantly, the value that agents bring to their customers is actually hard to define, especially because they make no coverage rules and essentially tell customers what's covered, what's not and how they should follow the carriers' rules. Agents have no financial incentive to challenge carriers on behalf of their clients. They're therefore not client advocates. The so-called independent agents are also stuck in the buttered–bread syndrome. If present trends continue, insurance agents will disappear about the same time we bury the last baby boomers.

Realtors

This industry is also under attack from companies such as *OpenListings* and the larger *for-sale-by-owner* (FSBO) community. But the traditional players have some powerful friends that lobby endlessly to keep their hold on how real estate is bought and sold. There are so many hands in the typical transaction that it's impossible to even identify all of the financial vested interests in real estate transactions—which makes the industry difficult to attack. Here's a point of view (Kasanoff, 2016):

> I'd like to suggest that 95% of a broker's role could be handled better by well-designed technology systems. Bidding, for example, could be handled by an automated system that includes legally-binding documents that would be instantly accessible to each party's attorney.

> Online bidding could enable buyers and sellers to learn much more about the others' interests and needs; in many cases brokers play games

with such information, either holding it back or deliberately distorting it to better produce the outcomes they desire.

For example, I'd like all potential sellers to know that I can be extremely flexible with my closing dates, should they still need to find a new property to buy. It would be great if they knew that up to a certain price point I can be a cash buyer, and that the absolute most I can pay is X.

The hardest broker role to replace is the one that adds the least value: letting buyers into a property. For obvious reasons, sellers do not want strangers walking around their homes alone. But the role of opening the door could be handled by a person earning perhaps $15 an hour, rather than someone who will take $50,000 from a $1 million transaction.

The fact is that one thing keeps the broker's role alive today: the regulations that govern the real estate industry. Once upon a time they might have been designed to protect consumers, but today they mainly protect realtors.

The disintermediation of real estate agents is more complicated than forcing cab drivers off the road. The buying and selling of property is a giant revenue stream for millions of players who all wet their beaks the second a transaction closes. There are regulatory constraints that make it difficult to disrupt the industry, but with the size of the revenue stream in play it's only a matter of time and initiative.

Banks

We have no idea why there are physical banks, human tellers, or what we carry around as money. Do you? According to Brett King, the founder of Moven (as reported by Eric Rosenbaum, 2015):

> The biggest banks in the world in 2025 will be technology companies, and banks that grew through branch acquisitions in the '80s and '90s that grew by physical bank presence, will have a real problem.

The trends are clear:

> Since 2011, 700 million global consumers have begun banking on their phone. The U.S. bank branch model, which peaks at a total of roughly 95,000 branches, is now down to 86,000 branches.

Money is also disappearing. *Way back in 2012*, Jacey Fortin reported that:

> In Sweden, monetary transactions made with physical cash are down to three percent of the national economy ... in most Swedish cities, public buses don't accept cash; tickets are prepaid or purchased with a cell phone text message, reports AP. A small but growing number of businesses only take cards, and some bank offices—which make money on electronic transactions—have stopped handling cash altogether. This looks like the beginning of a global trend; people everywhere are noticing that physical cash is becoming less and less common.

Merryn Somerset Webb reported that Denmark quickly followed:

> The Danish government is concerned that cash puts too many "administrative and financial burdens" on shops and that it acts as a drag on GDP growth. So, as part of a wide group of proposals to boost economic growth, it is to allow shops to stop taking cash. This makes sense in all sorts of ways. As M&G's Jim Leaviss points out, handling cash is expensive—you have to process it, give people change for it, provide security for it, take it to the bank, etc. Cash is also a bore for governments because it is the main facilitator of the black economy—anything paid for via the banking system can be taxed; anything paid for in cash can be missed. Plus, physical cash often means physical crime, so getting rid of cash could mean less crime and less tax evasion.

The U.S. lags but it's only a matter of time and money, especially because of the control that cashless transactions provide governments and the financial gains banks accrue from closing their branches and going cashless.

Professionals

There's no need for so many physical, organic, living and breathing professionals in the digital era. Expertise defined around *rules* can be automated and distributed at the touch of a key, a verbal command, or a reasonably intelligent assistant. Automated reasoning will replace many lawyers, doctors, accountants, professors and engineers.

But it's not just knowledge-based professions at risk. Manufacturing, production and transactional professions are also at risk. According to National Public Radio (NPR) research as reported by Ben Snyder (2015):

> Telemarketers' jobs have the highest chance of being automated ... other positions with huge potential for being overtaken by robots? Cashiers, tellers and drivers, among others, according to this new NPR interactive. While telemarketers have a 99% chance of one day being totally replaced by technology (it's already happening), cashiers, tellers and drivers all have over a 97% chance at being automated. Many positions within the "production" category put together by NPR, including packaging and assembly jobs, tend to rank highly as well.

This means that technology will disrupt knowledge- *and* production-based professions and the fields that prepare and maintain these professionals. Note that trickle-down disruption will be much more impactful than first-order disruption.

Politics

Social media represents the tip of the political iceberg. Every time Donald Trump tweets something, and every time someone responds, there's someone in the media or academia that notes the importance of digital politics. But the long-term impact that digital technology will have on politics will be profound—and controversial. Imagine, for example, how registration/voting-by-phone would affect voter registration and election outcomes? The discussions about voter registration and voter rights would disappear—which is why there's a major clash between digital technology and democratic politics.

There are security issues that must still be resolved before universal, global Internet voting (regardless of the device used to cast the vote) becomes routine. But given the growing dependency on digital technology in all aspects of industry and government, it's impossible to believe that security concerns will prevent the consummation of politics and technology. The real constraints are likely to be political, not technological, though technology may well become the scapegoat to objections to fully digitize the political process. All of that said, imagine the efficiencies around immediate communications, referenda and elections. It is inevitable.

So What?

We have seen whole industries disrupted by digital technology over the past two decades. But all of that disruption combined only represents Disruption 1.0. The five industries discussed earlier represent just the beginning of Disruption 2.0. Similar to the *iPhone*, there are likely to be many incarnations over time. As machines get smaller, smarter and cheaper, we'll see more and more industries disrupted by digital professionals and their digital tools. The implications of continuous disruption are extensive and unpredictable. The world as we think we know it will never be, just as it never was.

The Innovation Challenge

Everyone likes to talk about DARPA's approach to innovation (Dugan and Gabriel, 2013). DARPA brought us the Internet, drones, global positioning and a bunch of other very cool stuff that arguably enabled the entire digital revolution. For many of us, DARPA defines innovation excellence.

But are DARPA's processes easily replicable?

Not easily.

The innovation lessons one takes away from DARPA are nearly impossible for private corporations to implement: just too many things have to be true for corporate innovation to work—and they seldom are. Before we begin, let's exclude companies such as Apple, Google and Samsung where innovation is a well-funded core competency.

The aspects of their innovation processes and culture are DARPA-like. But when most companies try to innovate, they fail miserably and almost always tend to eventually be disrupted by start-ups, such as LegalZoom, Amazon, or Uber (which themselves eventually face innovation challenges). This is an ongoing threat to successful digital transformation.

We focus here on companies that already have market share, already make money and already believe that they're *good* companies destined for continued greatness. Many of the executives and share-holders of these companies are already rich and (therefore) risk averse. The innovative teams that made them rich are long since gone. Autopilot is a good way to think about many companies—until their revenue and profit falls. Some examples? JC Penny, Sunoco, Research in Motion, Red Lobster, McDonald's and Major League Baseball. These companies often try to innovate but end up following rather than leading especially when it comes to digital innovation.

So let's start with motivation.

DARPA program managers are motivated by *before-and-after*-fame and *after-cool-fortune*. Really smart people are given big budgets to do amazing things. They perform because (1) they're taxpayer funded, because (2) there's a world-class DARPA ecosystem (DARPA, its DOD test clients and its industry and university partners) that rewards cool stuff and (3) because once the ecosystem nods approval, DARPA professionals get to monetize their success with university positions, university grants, high paying industry positions, and if they choose, other government positions with greater budgets and power. It's a well-understood motivational model—with minimal risk to the innovators or the sponsors.

If their ideas actually turn out to be cool, there's a lot of personal fame in the process too. Many DARPA program managers love technological fame, and there's no shortage of fame to go around.

Implied in the DARPA innovation model is the acceptability of failure, because, let's be honest, it's taxpayers' money and because no one gets it right every time. So failing is acceptable, not just because it's part of the culture, but because failure is a non-zero-sum game: blowing a few million on a failed project doesn't take a nickel out of my—or my boss's—pocket. If the program manager loses $25 million, the same thing is true—but not in industry: everyone notices a $25,000,000 write-off—and if someone does it a few times, *they're* written off (unless they're someone's best friend, of course).

Motivating beyond the obvious—compensation and stock—is tough for most companies to understand. It's also tough for companies to actually approve failure, even though they usually state for the record that they're willing to risk millions on innovative efforts—even if they fail. Corporate innovators are financially and politically constrained from the moment they get the innovation assignment.

Motivation and money are intertwined. Money creates freedom. At DARPA, ideas must be pitched to office directors and the director of the agency. The working premise is that there's always money to pursue what a very small number of people believe are good ideas. The nonsense we hear all the time that funding follows good ideas is ridiculous: *the best innovation cultures assume the opposite, that there's a pile of cash just waiting to be spent, that will be spent on something, that there's no groveling for pilot project funding that may or may not lead to Phase 2.* No SWOT charting, please. Such tools are designed to reduce risk, not to innovate: if your company passes ideas through elaborate SWOT filters, it's not innovating. Put another way, innovation is not reactive, staged or managed. It's proactive and unwieldy with poorly defined and ideally unanticipated, though impactful, outcomes, if you're lucky. Yes, *lucky*. Never discount the role that luck plays in the innovation process, though *luck* is an expensive attribute of innovation.

Most companies have a really tough time prefunding ill-defined innovation. Most companies want to manage *innovation the way they manage the construction of a new factory. It seldom, if ever, works. Most companies despise the idea of investing in luck.*

At DARPA, really smart people rotate in an out of the agency. Typically, they're already part of the DARPA ecosystem. They've generally proven their value from high profile scientific, engineering, or technology projects—their passport into the ecosystem. If you turn out to be *relatively* unintelligent at DARPA, you're marginalized. You can fail, but you must be smart. Many companies, on the other hand, frequently reward style over substance, relationships over performance. Sometimes the innovation *assignment* is even given to long-standing corporate cronies. The idea of taking the best and brightest salespersons, supply chain managers, or customer service experts, and giving them a DARPA-like 2-to-3 year assignment to just think about new ways to do old things worries stock chaperones to no end. So, the in-house corporate innovation team is often mediocre and therefore destined to fail.

Most companies find it difficult if not impossible to grant sabbaticals to groups of hi-po's (high potentials)—or even lo-po's, for that matter. They want to keep them on-the-line generating profits when it's precisely the best and the brightest that should own innovation.

DARPA loves small teams, sometimes comprised of a single scientist, engineer, or technologist (with some supporting members from the ecosystem). Big companies love big teams with explicit governance about who gets to say and do what/when/where. Many DARPA professionals are intellectually arrogant. In fact, they paid to misbehave. Discussions where geniuses crush merely intelligent people happen all the time. Most companies don't like this kind of dialog—at least face-to-face: most corporate battles are fought behind the scenes where clever people leverage their tenured relationships and personal styles to get what they want. DARPA is much more of a meritocracy than most companies, regardless of how companies might perceive or describe themselves. In fact, the assumption at DARPA is that individuals can often carry the innovation load all by themselves, though obviously the DARPA ecosystem is continuously leveraged.

Most companies would never trust a huge innovation budget with one person, regardless of how smart, glib, or connected they were. Most companies would never allow innovation efforts to just float out there over long periods of time with no governance. Companies need to control budgets, people and processes—which is why they usually fail so spectacularly at innovation.

Innovation is not a set of activities; it's an attitude, a culture, supported by a set of loose processes and even less-defined outcomes. Most corporate cultures are therefore, by definition, anything but innovative. In fact, corporate cultures are designed to be repeatable, consistent, predictable and profitable. They're also designed to be scalable, but only within limits.

Self-disruption is not a competency many companies have, which is why most innovation is de facto or de jure outsourced to those with separate vested financial interests. It's also nearly impossible for successful companies to cannibalize their revenue streams, even if there's consensus that the streams are not permanent. Print media, for example, still double downs on print-driven business models, while just about everyone knows that the death of print media correlates perfectly with the rising death rate of today's consumers of print media.

So, how many innovation consultants can one company hire?

Can they survive in corporate cultures that talk one innovation game but play another?

The argument here is simple. Successful companies become successful because they optimize routines in relatively stable markets, not because they continuously search for new ways to replace old, profitable processes or when they should eliminate profitable SKUs because *it's time*. The financial corporate structure is biased against innovation. They're convinced that they can *reengineer*, *reinvent* and *innovate* at will when nothing could be further from the truth. They almost always need a lot of outside help to change processes, products and services, and even when there's help, they usually fail.

Very few will ever become DARPA-like.

Wake up, Smell the Technology and Transform

We conclude this book with a discussion around innovation challenges. Although DARPA-like innovation structures and processes are hard to replicate, they're precisely what *ideal* digital transformation requires. Our data suggest that companies are modifying their structures and processes already—which is a huge step in the right direction. DARPA-like innovation assumes speed and discovery. Corporate digital transformation through rapid technology adoption assumes speed *and* discovery. Although (DARPA) government and corporate motivations are different, they're ultimately about competition. DARPA worries about *global* adversaries, whereas companies worry about disruptive *corporate* adversaries.

The key is commitment. Companies that think proactively–that try to anticipate futures–will commit to transformation and adopt emerging and disruptive technologies opportunistically—and quickly. If they lag—such as the *laggards* of the twentieth century—they will fail. But if they're proactive, their transformations will be significant.

Appendix A: Technology Adoption Survey

To test our hypotheses and answer our questions, we posted the following survey:

- How is technology *organized and governed* at your company?
  - Centralized (under a CIO/CTO at the enterprise/corporate level)
  - Federated (shared with the business units with BU technology leadership)
  - Decentralized (limited or no technology controls)
  - Hybrid technology governance model
  - Not sure
- Do you have a *defined process for adopting emerging/disruptive technology* in place?
  - Yes
  - No
  - Not sure
- Is your organization a requirements-first/technology-second *or a* technology-first/requirements-second organization?
  - Requirements first/technology second

- Technology first/requirements second
- Neither
- Not sure

- To what extent do *Shadow IT* organizations and *Shadow IT* spending influence the technology adoption process at your company? (*Shadow IT* is technology spending and deployment that is *unauthorized* by the corporate IT)
  - A lot
  - Some
  - Very little
  - Not at all

- Does your company have a *formal requirements analysis/ validation/management/SDLC-like methodology in place?*
  - Yes
    - If *yes*, which one?
      - Systems development life cycle (SDLC)
      - Rapid application development (RAD)
      - Open-source development
      - Object-oriented programming
      - Joint applications development (JAD)
      - Software prototyping
      - Extreme programming (XP)
      - Agile

- Has your company *adopted technology*—or even baskets of technologies—*without any specific problems or applications in mind?*
  - Often
  - Occasionally
  - Sometimes
  - Never

- How comfortable is your organization with the approach *that assumes that technologies can, and often should, drive requirements even before requirements are defined?*
  - Very
  - Somewhat
  - Not at all

- Does your organization maintain an *ongoing list of* promising, *emerging and potentially disruptive technologies?*
  - Yes
  - No
  - Sometimes
  - Don't know
- *Which emerging/disruptive technologies* do you believe have great potential (all that apply)?
  - Cloud services?
    - Infrastructure-as-a-Service
    - Software-as-a-Service
    - Platform-as-a-Service
    - Security-as-a-Service
    - Data-as-a-Service
    - Mobility-as-a-Service
    - Hardware-as-a-Service
    - Analytics-as-a-Service
  - Private cloud?
    - Yes
    - No
  - Public cloud?
    - Yes
    - No
  - Hybrid public/private cloud?
    - Yes
    - No
  - Social media listening and engagement?
    - Internal (employee) corporate social media listening
    - External (customers) social media listening
    - External social media engagement
    - No
  - Big data analytics
    - Structured data analytics (sales, customers, manufacturing, etc. ...)
    - Unstructured data analytics (social media, call centers, e-Mail, etc. ...)

- Integrated (structured and unstructured) data analytics
- Descriptive analytics
- Predictive analytics
- Prescriptive analytics

- Cryptocurrencies
  - Yes
  - No
- e-Payment systems
  - Yes
  - No
- Security technologies
  - Secure hyper text transfer protocol
  - Transport layer security
  - Private key encryption
  - Hardware tokens
  - Mobile application wrappers
  - Virtual desktop containers
  - APT detection, analysis
  - Mobile device management
  - Crowdsourced threat protection and analysis
  - Multifactor/multilevel user authentication
  - Biometric multilevel authentication (including finger-prints, voice recognition and other biometrics)
  - Updated identity, access management systems
  - Decoys and honeypots...
- e-Learning (online) systems for employee training
  - Yes
  - No
  - Don't know
- Bring-your-own-devices (BYODs)
  - Yes
  - No
  - A little
  - Don't know
- 3D printing
  - Yes

- No
- Don't know
- Proprietary mobile video-conferencing systems (e.g., Cisco)
  - Yes
  - No
  - Don't know
- Open source mobile video-conferencing systems (e.g., Skype)
  - Yes
  - No
  - Don't know
- Advanced human–computer interfaces
  - Speech-to-speech
  - Gesture control
  - Biometric-based interfaces
  - Don't know...
- Wearable devices
  - Yes
  - No
  - Don't know
- Internet-of-Things (IoT)
  - Yes
  - No
  - Don't know
- Location-based services
  - Yes
  - No
  - Don't know
- Virtual reality and augmented reality
  - Yes
  - No
  - Don't know
- Drones
  - Yes
  - No
  - Don't know

- Automated reasoning/artificial intelligence/cognitive computing
  - Yes
  - No
  - Don't know
- *How do you hear about emerging/disruptive technologies* (all that apply)?
  - From in-house technology experts
  - From in-house business experts
  - From consultants
  - From vendors
  - From your personal network (friends, family, etc.)
  - From research organizations (Gartner, Cutter, Forester, IDC, etc. …)
- What are the *drivers of your emerging/disruptive technology adoption* (check all that apply)?
  - Competitive fear
  - Consumer product awareness (e.g., iPads)
  - Pressure from the business units
  - Pressure from line management
  - Pressure from senior management
  - Pressure from the C-suite
  - Opportunities for digital transformation
  - Opportunities to reduce costs…
- Where is your company or business unit *along the emerging technology adoption curve*?
  - Innovator
  - Early adopter
  - Early majority
  - Late majority
  - Laggard

We then presented the same list to survey respondents and asked which of the technologies on the list they intended to pilot in 2016.

Appendix B: Interview Questions and Selected Responses

Selected Questions

- *Are you still anchored in* requirements-first/technology-second *technology adoption processes?*
- *What would happen if you threw the SDLC out the window— and just brought all kinds of new technologies into the company and started to pilot them?*
- *What examples do you have of successful and unsuccessful emerging technology pilots and deployments?*
- *In your view, are technologies/platforms/devices like iPads, social media and analytics ready to go?*
- *What worries you about early/almost immediate technology adoption?*
- *How much Shadow IT is there at your company? Does Shadow IT fuel emerging technology adoption? Should you shut it down? Or should you let it go?*
- *What new/emerging/ready/disruptive technologies are high on your list? Which ones do you think have been overhyped?*

- *Do you think that the era of huge, proprietary platforms—like ERP, CRM and DBMS platforms—is over? That it's now possible to integrate* pieces *of applications that used to be in a single platform through cloud SaaS providers?*
- *Do you think that* consumerization—*the adoption of emerging technology by consumers—has forever changed the business technology adoption process?*
- *Are rapid adoption experiences anomalies or precedents?*

Selected Responses

A CEO from a mid-sized pharmaceutical company: "We have to use whatever technology we can to stay competitive. I really don't care where it comes from. If it helps me I will try it. Years ago I had to ask permission to try a new technology. Can you imagine? I'm the CEO. It's because we put in place governance rules that centralized tech in one department ... in one guy ... made no sense then and make less sense now. Yes, we adopt technology as fast as we can if it can help us make more money ..."

A CIO from a health care insurance company: "Our role has changed. We no longer tell business units what they can and cannot do. They are under a new directive: go forth and make money. So we play the role of vetter. We want to make sure that the technology they pilot and deploy is safe and supportable—not by us, but by someone usually in the cloud ..."

Business analyst in a real estate brokerage: "We're always worried about nontraditional competitors. At some point technology will change the role of the real estate agent. We track that technology closely. We pilot everything we see that might impact the real estate transaction process. Requirements? We know what we require. We don't need to spend a year defining it."

Financial services COO: "IT has ruled the roost for years. We let them. Now I have professionals coming up to me asking about smartphone apps, backups to personal clouds and how we service customers with mobile apps. We try things all the time. In the old days, we didn't even tell 'IT' what we were doing.

We just did it. Now we still just do it and now we tell them if they're even interested."

CFO of an e-Retailer: "Even I know the world is changing and that technology is the change agent. I also know that in order to remain competitive we need to move fast—especially because market forces are pushing us. Technologies like mobile payment systems, cryptocurrencies, Bitcoin, analytics and digital security measures are all important. I'm sure you're surprised at what I just said. I'm a CFO! But even I know the technologies that can make us great or kill us. This is where we live in 2016."

Marketing officer at a large technology vendor: "Cloud delivery has changed the world. We used to make tons of money selling huge applications to unsuspecting clients. We made money, the implementation consultants made money and the clients had no choice but to stay the course. But now clients are asking for cloud delivery options. They also want cheaper, faster, better all the time—and when we can't deliver they go elsewhere, sometimes even to their home IT departments! They also go to social media and other media to understand what we are selling and what people like or hate about our products or services."

Director at a specialty pharmaceuticals company: "We're all about 'new.' When iPads were released we bought hundreds of them to play with. We do the same thing when new technology is released that might help us innovate, manufacture or sell—and the count the money. IT is 'there,' but its role is different now. It makes sure that email works and the networks stay up, but IT doesn't tell us what to do. We do what we want. That will never change. *The Genie's out of the bottle. Tech moves too fast.* Requirements chase technologies that actually tell us how we can use them to solve problems."

IT manager at a telecommunications company: "SDLC? I have no idea what that even is. We don't develop software applications from the ground up anymore. We might customize some applications on cloud platforms—like Salesforce—but not with our own large development teams. Those days are over—and gone forever. Why in the world would we hire programmers when we can rent applications from the cloud?"

Appendix C: Statistical Tests

The analyses we performed might contain sampling errors due to the limited nature of our dataset. While our goal was to understand the *big picture* of the relationship between the different variables in our survey and the adoption rate of emerging technologies, we nevertheless employed various statistical techniques such as k-fold cross-validation, Fisher's exact test and boosted neural networks to mitigate some of the biases that might be in the data.

We wanted to discover which variables in the survey affected the rate of emerging technology adoption; we used the statistical software package, SAS JMP Pro. We defined the fast-emerging technology adopters as respondents who answered either *within a month of learning about them* or *within six months of learning about them*. The other answers such as *within a year after learning about them, more than a year after learning about them* and *we have not had and have no plans to have such pilots* are classified as slow adopters. *In other words, we classified respondents who piloted or planned to pilot emerging/disruptive technologies within six months of learning about them as rapid adopters, and the rest as slow adopters.*

To better understand the underlying factors between the two different groups, we performed a contingency analysis on the different categorical responses to the survey questions with the classification. To determine whether a response to each one of our survey questions is statistically different between the two classification groups, we used Fisher's exact test. We opted for this statistical significance test with our limited dataset because Fisher's exact test is independent of sample size (Fisher, 1922).

Using Fisher's exact test, we performed a test of independence on each survey question and the adoption classification. Our testing was as follows:

H_0: *The answer to the survey and the adoption classification are independent*

H_A: *The answer to the survey and the adoption classification are not independent*

At α level of 5%, we can conclude that these six questions have some association with the adoption classification.

1. How comfortable is your organization with the approach that assumes technologies can, and often should, drive requirements even before requirements are defined?
2. Does your organization maintain an ongoing list of *promising*, emerging and potentially disruptive technologies?
3. Where is your company or business unit along the emerging technology adoption curve?
4. Has your company or business unit abandoned or modified the (*Early*, *Late*, *Laggard*, etc.) traditional technology adoption model?
5. Are there professionals at your company who specialize in the rapid prototyping of emerging/disruptive technologies?
6. Does your company quantitatively measure the success/failure of emerging/disruptive technology pilots?

QUESTION NUMBER	STATISTICAL SIGNIFICANCE (FISHER'S EXACT TEST)
1	0.004
2	0.0419
3	0.0179
4	0.0203
5	0.0153
6	0.0031

Fisher's Exact Test on Survey Questions

Questions 1 and 6 are highly statistically significant. It seems that the comfort level companies have with technology driving requirements and quantitatively measuring the success/failure of emerging technology pilots have a high impact on how fast companies adopt emerging technology.

Intuitively, these results pass the smell test. It's obvious that some of these variables such as having a dedicated emerging technology team for pilots and maintaining a list of emerging technologies could have a significant impact on how fast companies pilot emerging technologies: having people whose sole job it is to pilot the latest and greatest emerging technologies can affect how fast companies pilot them.

We went a step further to discover how answers to each question affect the outcome of the adoption classification by using several analytical techniques such as Naïve Bayes classification, logistical regression, artificial neural networks and multiple correspondence analysis: we sought to build a prediction model using the variables we have.

Due to the limited nature of our dataset, we found that using artificial neural networks to build our predictive model gave us the best results. We used the k-fold cross-validation method to validate our results to minimize data wastage and overfitting the data. Here are the results of the model.

After several iterations, we developed a model that had a misclassification rate of only 5.7% for the training dataset and an even lower rate of 3.8% for our validation dataset. That said, due to our small sample size, our model might not reference all of the variability in the general population.

Training Dataset	
Measures	**Value**
Generalized RSquare	0.7907299
Entropy RSquare	0.6667708
RMSE	0.2281668
Mean absolute deviation	0.1655867
Misclassification rate	0.0571429
Log likelihood	21.51286
Sum frequency	105

Validation Dataset	
Measures	**Value**
Generalized RSquare	0.7180889
Entropy RSquare	0.5849098
RMSE	0.2586073
Mean absolute deviation	0.1939231
Misclassification rate	0.0384615
Log likelihood	6.2864581
Sum frequency	26

Confusion Matrix

Actual	Predicted Rate	
Adoption Rate	Greater than 6 months or no plans	Less than 6 months
Greater than 6 months or no plans	27	5
Less than 6 months	1	72

Confusion Matrix

Actual	Predicted Rate	
Adoption Rate	Greater than 6 months or no plans	Less than 6 months
Greater than 6 months or no plans	7	0
Less than 6 months	1	18

Confusion Rates

Actual	Predicted Rate	
Adoption Rate	Greater than 6 months or no plans	Less than 6 months
Greater than 6 months or no plans	0.844	0.156
Less than 6 months	0.014	0.986

Confusion Rates

Actual	Predicted Rate	
Adoption Rate	Greater than 6 months or no plans	Less than 6 months
Greater than 6 months or no plans	1	0
Less than 6 months	0.053	0.947

Training Dataset

Validation Dataset

Artificial neural networks, while lauded for their predictive capabilities, are also known for their *black box* (Benitez et al., 1997) when interpreting the results of the model. We attempted to circumvent this apparent difficulty in interpretation by utilizing JMP's built in categorical prediction profiler which enhanced the interpretability of our model (Figure C.1).

Using the profiler, we simulated answers to the six questions that we identified previously and predicted a possible classification for the scenario. We also analyzed how each factor/variable affected the prediction outcome (Figure C.2).

We can see that the most important factor (Sobol', 1993; Saltelli, 2002) in our prediction model was whether a company measures the success of their emerging technology pilots (48% of variability) followed by their position on the adoption curve (34% of variability): it seems that being comfortable with technology driving requirements before business requirements are defined is the least important factor (21% of variability) (Figure C.3).

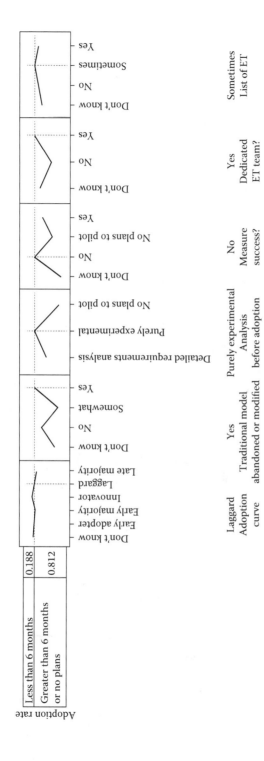

Figure C.1   An example of the profiler.

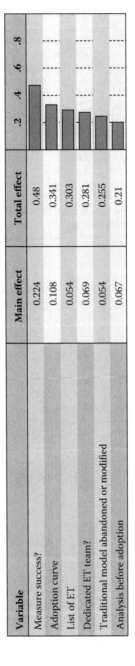

Variable	Main effect	Total effect	.2	.4	.6	.8
Measure success?	0.224	0.48				
Adoption curve	0.108	0.341				
List of ET	0.054	0.303				
Dedicated ET team?	0.069	0.281				
Traditional model abandoned or modified	0.054	0.255				
Analysis before adoption	0.067	0.21				

Figure C.2   Variable importance: Independent resampled inputs.

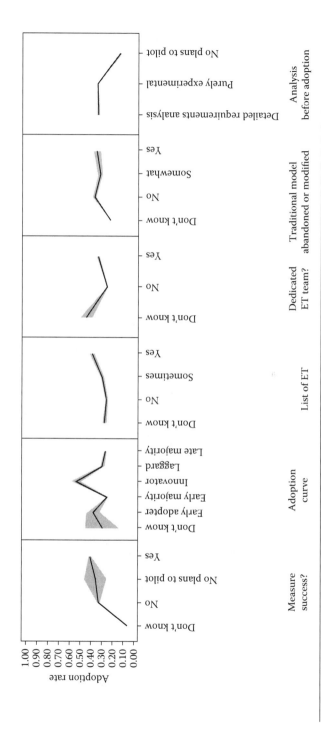

Figure C.3   Marginal model plots.

We can see how the answers to each question affect the likelihood of piloting an emerging technology within 6 months. The y-axis (Adoption Rate) closer than 1 is analogous to increasing probability that the company will pilot an emerging technology within 6 months of knowing about it.

Bibliography

Agarwal, R., G. Gao, C. DesRoches, and A.K. Jha. (2010). The digital transformation of healthcare: Current status and the road ahead. *Information Systems Research*, 21 (4), 796–809.

Agarwal, R. and V. Sambamurthy. (2002). Principles and models for organizing the information technology function. *Management Information Systems Quarterly Executive*, 1 (1), 1–16.

Andal-Ancion, A., P.A. Cartwright, and G.S. Yip. (2003). The digital transformation of traditional business. *Sloan Management Review*, 44 (4), 34–41.

Andriole, S.J. (1986). *Software Validation, Verification, Testing, and Documentation.* Princeton, NJ: Petrocelli Books.

Andriole, S.J. (1987). Storyboard prototyping for requirements verification. *Large Scale Systems*, 12 (3), 231–247.

Andriole, S.J. (1989). *Storyboard Prototyping: A New Approach to User Requirements Analysis.* Wellesley, MA: QED Information Sciences.

Andriole, S.J. (1992). *Rapid Applications Prototyping: The Storyboard Approach to User Requirements Analysis.* Wellesley, MA: QED Information Sciences.

Andriole, S.J. (1996). *Managing Systems Requirements: Methods, Tools & Cases.* New York: McGraw-Hill.

Andriole, S.J. (2007). The 7 habits of highly effective technology leaders. *Communications of the ACM*, 50 (3), 66–72.

Andriole, S.J. (2009). Cloud computing. *The Cutter IT Journal: The Journal of Information Technology Management.*

Andriole, S.J. (2010). Business technology strategy in the early 21st century: Optimization through rationalization. *Journal of Information Technology Research.*

Andriole, S.J. (2012a). 7 indisputable trends that will define 2015. *Communications of the AIS*, 30.

Andriole, S.J. (2012b). *IT's All about the People: Technology Management That Overcomes Disaffected People, Stupid Processes, and Deranged Corporate Cultures*. Boca Raton, FL: CRC Press.

Andriole, S.J. (2012c). Managing technology in a 2.0 world. *IEEE IT Professional*, 14, 50–57.

Andriole, S.J. (2013). Out of the gate & running wild. *Cutter Journal of Information Technology*, 26.

Andriole, S.J. (2014a). Ready technology. *Communications of the ACM*, 57 (2), 40–42.

Andriole, S.J. (2014b). *Ready Technology: Fast Tracking New Business Technologies*. Boca Raton, FL: Taylor & Francis Group.

Andriole, S.J. (2015). Who owns IT? *Communications of the ACM*, 58 (3), 28–30.

Andriole, S.J. (2017a). 5 myths of digital transformation. *Sloan Management Review*.

Andriole, S.J. (2017b). 15 must have skillsets for digital transformation. *European Business Review*.

Andriole, S.J. and L. Adelman. (1995). *Cognitive Systems Engineering for User-Computer: Interface Design, Prototyping, and Evaluation*. Hillsdale, NJ: Lawrence Erlbaum Associates.

Bass, F.M. (1969). A new product growth model for consumer durables. Lecture Notes in Economics and Mathematical Systems Mathematical Models in Marketing. *Management Science*, 15, 215–227.

Benítez, J.M., J.L. Castro, and I. Requena. (1997). Are artificial neural networks black boxes? *IEEE Transactions on Neural Networks*, 8, 1156–1164.

Bloch, M., S. Blumberg, and J. Laatz. (2012). *Delivering Large-scale IT Projects on Time, on Budget, and on Value*. McKinsey & Company.

Bloomberg, J. (2014). Digital transformation by any other name? *Forbes Magazine*, July 31.

Boehm, B.W. (1988). A spiral model of software development and enhancement. *Computer*, 21 (5), 61–72.

Bresciani, S. and M. Eppker. (2016). Gartner's magic quadrant and hype cycle. ResearchGate, University Della Svizzera Italiana, 2012.

Brooks, F. (1987). No silver bullet: Essence and accidents of software engineering. *Computer*, 20 (4), 10–19.

Brown, A.E. and G.G. Grant. (2005). Framing the frameworks: A review of IT governance re-search. *Communications of the AIS*, 15 (38), 696–712.

Brown, C.V. and S.L. Magill. (1994). Alignment of the IS functions with the enterprise: Toward a model of antecedents. *MIS Quarterly*, 18 (4), 371–403.

Carr, N. (2003). IT doesn't matter. *Harvard Business Review*, May.

Carr, N. (2004). *Does IT matter?* Boston, MA: Harvard Business School Press.

Carmel, E. and P. Abbott. (2006). Configurations of global software development: Offshore versus nearshore, in *Proceedings of the 2006 International Workshop on Global Software Development for the Practitioner, International Conference on Software Engineering*.

Chan, Y.E. and B.H. Reich. (2007). IT alignment: What have we learned. *Journal of Information Technology*, 22, 297–315.

Chandrasekaran, D. and G.J. Tellis. (2007). A critical review of marketing research on diffusion of new products. *Review of Marketing Research*, 3, 39–80.

Charette, R.N. (2012). US air force blows $1 billion on failed ERP project. *IEEE Spectrum*, November.

Christensen, C. (1997). *The Innovator's Dilemma*. Harvard Business Review Press.

Christensen, C.M. (2016). *The Innovator's Dilemma: When New Technologies Cause Great Firms to Fail*. Boston, MA: Harvard Business Review.

Christensen, C.M. and M.E. Raynor. (2013). *The Innovator's Solution: Creating and Sustaining Successful Growth*. Boston, MA: Harvard Business Review.

Constance Ledoux Book and D.A. Grady. Consumer adoption of new radio distribution systems, NAB Grant Report, June 2005.

Crandal, B., G. Klein, and R. Hoffman. (2006). *Working Minds: A Practitioner's Guide to Cognitive Task Analysis*. Cambridge, MA: MIT Press.

Currier, G. (2011). Emerging technology adoption trends in 2011. *CIO Insight*, January 3.

Davis, A.M. (1990). *Software Requirements: Analysis and Specification*. Englewood Cliffs, NJ: Prentice Hall.

Dorfman, M. and R.H. Thayer, Eds. (1997). *Software Requirements Engineering*. Los Alamitos, CA: IEEE Computer Society Press.

Dugan, R.E. and K.J. Gabriel. (2013). 'Special forces' innovation: How DARPA attacks problems. *Harvard Business Review*, October.

Evaristo, J.R., K.C. Desouza, and K. Hollister. (2005). Centralization momentum: The pendulum swings back again. *Communications of the ACM*, 48 (2), 67–71.

Faulk, S.R. (1997). Software requirements: A tutorial. In *Software Requirements Engineering*, R. Thayer and M. Dorfman (Eds.), pp. 128–149. Los Alamitos, CA: IEEE Computer Society Press.

Fenn, J. (2007). Understanding Gartner's hype cycles. Gartner Research, ID Number G00144727.

Fenn, J. and M. Raskino. (2008). *Mastering the Hype Cycle: How to Choose the Right Innovation at the Right Time*. Boston, MA: Harvard Business Press.

Fisher, R.A. (1922). On the interpretation of χ^2 from contingency tables, and the calculation of P. *Journal of the Royal Statistical Society*, 85 (1), 87–94.

Font, V.M. (2014). Who's to blame for troubled projects, IT or the business? UltimateSDLC.com. *The Ultimate Guide to the SDLC*, December.

Fortin, J. (2012). Sweden going cashless: Pros and cons of paper money. *International Business Times*, May 27.

Gartner Group. (2015). Gartner identifies the top 10 strategic technology trends for 2015, October 8.

Gartner Group. (2016). Gartner's 2016 hype cycle for emerging technologies identifies three key trends that organizations must track to gain competitive advantage, August 16.

Gens, F. (2014). *IDC Predictions 2015: Accelerating Innovation - and Growth - on the 3rd Platform.* IDC.

Ghobakhloo, M., T. Hong, M. Sabouri, and N. Zulkifli. (2012). Strategies for successful information technology adoption in small and medium-sized enterprises. *Information*, 3, 36–67.

Greene, K. (2005). Most important Infotech stories of '05, *MIT Technology Review*, December 30.

Hinkle, J. (2016). J&J warns diabetic patients: Insulin pump vulnerable to hacking. *Reuters*.

Horrigan, J. (2008). *Use of Cloud Computing Applications and Services.* Pew Internet & American Life Project.

IBM. (2016). *Millennials: The Insurance Customer Has Changed, Will You?*

Joyce, W., N. Nohria, and B. Roberson. (2003). *What (Really) Works: The 4 + 2 Formula for Sustained Business Success.* New York: HarperCollins Publishers.

Kasanoff, B. (2016). 10 Powerful ways to empower your employees. *Forbes Magazine*, March 24.

Kimberling, E. (2015). *Key Findings from the 2015 Report.* Denver, CO: Panorama Consulting.

Klein, G. (1999). *Sources of Power: How People Make Decisions.* Cambridge, MA: MIT Press.

Klinger, D., S.J. Andriole, L.G. Militello, L. Adelman, and G. Klein. (1993). *Designing for Performance: A Cognitive Systems Engineering Approach to Modifying an AWACS Human Computer Interface.* Fairborn, OH: Klein Associates.

Lee, J. (2014). 9 VERY scary ERP and ERP system implementation statistics. *ERP/VAR*, October.

Leffingwell, D. (1997). Calculating the return on investment from more effective requirements management. *American Programmer*, 10 (4), 13–16.

Leibowitz, J. (2016). IT project failures: What management can learn. *IEEE IT Professional*, April.

Lepore, J. (2015). What the gospel of innovation gets wrong. *The New Yorker*, March.

Lucas, H. (2014). Disrupting and transforming the university. *Communications of the ACM*, 57 (10), 32–35.

Lynch, J. (2015). *The Chaos Report.* The Standish Group.

Macvaugh, J. and F. Schiavone. (2010). Limits to the diffusion of innovation. *European Journal of Innovation Management*, 13 (2), 197–221.

Madan, A. (2015). 100 open source big data architecture papers for data professionals. *LinkedIn*, June.

Mahajan, V., E. Muller, and R.K. Srivastava. (1990). Determination of adopter categories by using innovation diffusion models. *Journal of Marketing Research*, 27 (1), 37–50.

Marchand, D.A. and J. Peppard. (2013). Why IT fumbles analytics. *Harvard Business Review*, January–February.

Massoud, K. and P.L. Stoneman. (1993). Rank, stock, order, and epidemic effects in the diffusion of new process technologies: An empirical model. *The RAND Journal of Economics*, 24 (4), 503–528.

McKinsey & Company. (2016). Digital America: A tale of the haves and have-mores. McKinsey Global Institute.

Meeker, M. (2015). *2015 Internet Trends Report*. Kleiner Perkins Caufield Byers.

Miranda, R.A., W.D. Casebeer, A.M. Hein, J.W. Judy, E.P. Krotkov, T.L. Laabs, J.E. Manzo et al. (2014). DARPA-funded efforts in the development of novel brain-computer interface technologies. *Journal of Neuroscience Methods*, 244, 52–67.

Mithas, S., A. Tafti, I. Bardhan, and J.M. Goh. (2012). The impact of IT investments on profits. *Sloan Management Review*, 53, 15.

MITRE Corporation. (2016). *Eliciting, Collecting, and Developing Requirements*.

Moore, G.A. (1991). *Crossing the Chasm: Marketing & Selling High Tech Products to Mainstream Customers*. New York: HarperCollins Publishers.

Mullany, M. (2016). 8 lessons from 20 years of hype cycle. *LinkedIn*, December 7.

Murugesan, S. (2009). Cloud computing: A new paradigm in IT. *Cutter Business Intelligence Executive Report*, 9 (2).

Niu, S.C. (2002). A stochastic formulation of the bass model of new-product diffusion. *Mathematical Problems in Engineering*, 8 (3), 249–263.

Orr, K. and A. Maher. (2009). Here comes cloud computing. *Cutter Consortium Business Technology Trends & Impacts Council Opinion*, 10 (1).

Peterson, R. (2004). Crafting information technology governance. *EDPACS - The EDP Audit, Control and Security Newsletter*, 32, 1–24.

Rider, R. (2015). There's a major long-term trend in the economy that isn't getting enough attention. *Business Insider/The Blackrock Blog*.

Rockart, J., M. Earl, and J. Ross. (1996). Eight imperatives for the new IT organization. *Sloan Management Review*, 38, 43–55.

Rogers, D. (2016). *The Digital Transformation Playbook*. Columbia Business University Press.

Rogers, E.M. (1962). *Diffusion of Innovations*. New York: Free Press.

Rosenbaum, E. (2015). Retail bank branch is doomed, and banks don't know it. *CNBC*.

Saltelli, A. (2002). Making best use of model valuations to compute sensitivity indices. *Computer Physics Communications*, 145, 280–297.

Snyder, B. (2015). These jobs are most likely to be taken by a computer. *Fortune*.

Sobol', I.M. (1993). Sensitivity analysis for non-linear mathematical models. *Mathematical Modeling & Computational Experiment*, 1, 407–414.

Society for Information Management. (2017). *IT Trends Study: Taking the Pulse of IT*. Mount Laurel, NJ: Society for Information Management.

Steinert, M. and L. Heifer. (2010). *Scrutinizing Gartner's Hype Cycle Approach*. Stanford, CA: Stanford University, Center for Design Research (CDR).

Steinert, M. and L. Heifer. (2016). A critical analysis of the Garner's hype cycle. *PICMET 2010 Proceedings*, July 18–22, Phuket, Thailand.

The Chaos Chronicles/Standish Group. (2004). https://www.standishgroup.com.

Tiwana, A., B. Konsynski, and N. Venkatraman. (2013). Information technology and organizational governance: The IT governance cube. *Journal of Management Information Systems (Special Issue)*, 30 (3), 7–12.

Townsend, K. (2015). Containers: The pros and the cons of these VM alternatives. *TechRepublic*, February.

Ullah, A. and R. Lai. (2013). Requirements engineering and business/IT alignment: Lessons learned. *Journal of Software*, 8 (1), 1–10.

United States Government Accountability Office. (2008). http://www.gao.gov/financial_pdfs/citizensguide2008.pdf.

Van den Bulte, C. and G.L. Lilien. (1997). Bias and systematic change in the parameter estimates of macro-level diffusion models. *Marketing Science*, 16 (4), 338–353.

Vaquero, L.M., L. Rodero-Merino, J. Caceres, and M. Linder. (2009). A break in the clouds: Towards a cloud definition. *ACM SIGCOMM Computer Communication Review*, 39 (1), 50–55.

Vedrashko, I. (2008). Media history through Gartner Hype Cycle Graphs: 1995–2008. *FutureLab*, August 29.

Wailgum, T. (2009). 10 famous ERP disasters, dustups and disappointments. *CIO Magazine*, March.

Webb, M.S. (2015). Denmark's new rules on cash mark the beginning of the end for physical money. *MoneyWeek*, December. http://moneyweek.com/merryns-blog/denmarks-new-rules-on-cash-mark-the-beginning-of-the-end-for-physical-money/.

Weill, P. and M. Broadbent. (1998). *Leveraging the New Infrastructure: How Market Leaders Capitalize on Information Technology*. Boston, MA: Harvard Business School Press.

Wiegers, K.E. (2003). *Software Requirements*. Redmond, WA: Microsoft Press.

Wikipedia. (2016). Digital transformation.

Wingfield, N. (2011). Once wary, Apple warms up to business market. *The New York Times*, November 15.

Woods, T. (2016). The innovator's dilemma: Narrow theory, widely applied. *Hype*, January.

Worthen, B. (2012). Start-ups emerge as tech vendors of choice. *The Wall Street Journal*, August.

Index

Note: Page numbers followed by f refer to figures, respectively.